I0423828

CONTENTS

FOREWORD

Since World War II, the relationship between Turkey and the United States has been characterized by complexity and flux; there have been periods of remarkable cooperation, even when significant disagreements existed. Relations between the two countries are never merely bilateral, for the two are also linked to the North Atlantic Treaty Organization (NATO) and the European Union (EU). The relationship between those two organizations is also complicated because of differing core purposes and somewhat differing memberships. Current Turkey-U.S. diplomatic and military relations are more strained than in recent years, but both countries recognize how vital it is to address issues of mutual importance.

In mid-2007 the Atlantic Council, Strategic Studies Institute, and German Marshall Fund of the United States jointly organized a conference to discuss the current state of U.S.-Turkish-EU ties and to consider how those relations might be repaired and enhanced. Participants included an impressive collection of diplomats, academics, and policy analysts with extensive knowledge and relevant experience. This conference report provides an overview of the enduring issues that must be addressed if Turkey-U.S. relations are to move beyond current roadblocks and begin to realize their full potential. Since the conference that served as the basis of this report took place, the political environment in Turkey has changed, and several of the issues, such as the use of Iraq as a staging area by Kurdish insurgents, have continued to evolve. Such dynamics reveal the importance of the ideas surfaced in each of the conference presentations and the need to continue addressing the issues identified.

Such work should prove valuable to policymakers of both countries in their efforts to improve this vital relationship.

DOUGLAS C. LOVELACE, JR.
Director
Strategic Studies Institute

CHAPTER 1

REBUILDING U.S.-TURKEY RELATIONS IN A TRANSATLANTIC CONTEXT

Frances G. Burwell

The relationship between Turkey and the United States stands at a critical juncture. The crises over the bases of Kurdish insurgents (the Partiya Karkeren Kurdistan or Kurdish Workers Party [PKK]) in northern Iraq and a recent congressional resolution recalling the Armenian genocide demonstrate the severe erosion that has occurred since the end of the Cold War. Recent top-level meetings in Ankara and Washington produced conciliatory rhetoric, but they did not prevent a Turkish ground incursion into northern Iraq in late February 2008, and whether they will prevent a reawakening of the congressional resolution next year is far from clear. President George W. Bush has promised new levels of intelligence sharing and military liaison, but unless there are rapid, concrete results, these steps are likely to seem rather meager assistance to those Turks who see the U.S. invasion of Iraq as having enabled a deadly PKK resurgence. The Bush administration does seem to have blocked further consideration of the congressional resolution on Armenian genocide, but only after tensions with the Turkish government escalated to extremely high levels.

For the moment, with the Turkish ground incursion having ended, both of these disputes appear to be in abeyance, but the more fundamental challenge remains. The U.S.-Turkey relationship has never recovered from the end of the Cold War. Washington and Ankara have not yet established a basis for a renewed partnership, and in the meantime many Turks have concluded that the United States no longer takes Turkish interests into account as an ally should. In fact, a recent Pew survey found that 64 percent of Turks view the United States as the greatest threat to Turkey, and only 9 percent of Turks have a positive view of the United States.

The United States and Turkey must find a new foundation for their relationship. While the Soviet threat which prompted their partnership has ended, the United States and Turkey still share many strategic interests, including fighting terrorism and ensuring stability in the wider Middle East region. To date, Ankara and Washington have found it difficult to work together in confronting those challenges, as the crisis over the PKK bases in Iraq amply demonstrates. Paradoxically, it is these issues—the fight against terrorism and the need for stability in the wider Middle East—that, along with energy security, offer the most opportunities for potential collaboration and thus the basis for a reinvigorated partnership.

The strains between Turkey and the United States have coincided with growing doubts about Turkey's eventual accession to the European Union (EU). Turkey's relationship with the EU has never been smooth, but after making significant progress toward meeting the accession criteria in 2004-05, Turkey now seems unable to quell doubts in Europe as to whether it will qualify even in 10-12 years. French President Nicholas Sarkozy has heightened tensions by making clear his fundamental opposition to Turkish membership. The November 2007 progress report of the European Commission highlighted the need for Turkey to revamp Article 301 of its constitution, which prohibits the criticism of "Turkishness," clearly an infringement of the Western ideal of free speech.

The Turkish government has said it will do so, but many more such reforms will be required before EU membership will be achieved. Turkey's frustration has been heightened further by the lack of action within the EU that address the long-standing Cyprus issue.[1]

Poor relations with the United States and uncertainty over EU membership have added more pressures to an already tense Turkish political situation. Turkey's domestic politics have become increasingly divisive during the last few years, as the emergence of the Justice and Development Party (AK Party or AKP) has coincided with the decline of traditional secular political parties and a reemergence of PKK terrorism. The AKP came out of the July 2007 elections in a stronger position and was able to elect Abdullah Gül as president (after failing to do so in the spring of 2007). But the new parliament also includes strong representation by the major nationalist parties and a number of Kurdish nationalist politicians. With the traditional opposition in a weaker position, the stage is set for even more polarization, especially given growing nationalist concerns about the reforms needed for EU accession.

This might seem an inauspicious time to launch a new U.S.-Turkey partnership, given that the success of that partnership may depend on Turkey's internal stability and relations with the EU. Yet these issues also require a more positive U.S.-Turkey partnership that will leave Turkey feeling less isolated from its allies. The U.S.-Turkey relationship, Turkey's internal political development, and potential Turkish accession to the European Union are thus inextricably linked. Moreover, the challenges faced by the United States, Turkey, and the EU—particularly the threat of terrorism and political instability throughout the broader Middle East—demand that they find a new basis for acting together now. Looking for constructive ways to meet those challenges could provide the focus and motivation for a new U.S.-Turkey relationship.

Washington and Ankara: Together Again?

U.S. and Turkish leaders recognize that the bilateral relationship is in trouble, and have pledged repeatedly to work toward improvement.[2] To achieve a stronger partnership, however, the first step must be to understand the limits of the past. Turkish-U.S. harmony during the Cold War was never as real as is now nostalgically imagined. That relationship was based primarily on narrow geopolitical considerations, specifically, Turkey's value as a strategically located piece of real estate that offered an opportunity for the United States and its allies to position themselves close to Russia's southern flank. U.S.-Turkish discussion was often about the use of airbases or stationing of military forces, while the relationship was largely managed by the Turkish defense forces and the U.S. Department of Defense. Turkey's political and economic development was often seen as secondary to its stability, and the United States was viewed as tolerant of the Turkish military's interference in politics.

While the demise of the Soviet Union seemed to reduce Turkey's strategic value to the United States, the terrorist attacks of September 11, 2001, created expectations that Turkey would regain its former salience, especially after the United Statees began to turn its sights on Saddam Hussein. The U.S. decision to invade Iraq, however, actually set back the realization of those hopes. The impending war was viewed with alarm in Turkey, and the U.S. request to open a second front through Turkey was rejected by the parliament in March 2003.

The war in Iraq has heightened Turkish fears of instability in the region and contributed to the precipitous drop in Turkish public support for the United States. On the U.S. side, Turkey's loyalty as an ally now seems less assured, even though major portions of U.S. equipment and personnel headed to Iraq continue to go through Incirlik Airbase. As the U.S. Government came to focus primarily on Iraq, attention to Turkey has become episodic.

In an effort to reenergize the relationship, the State Department and Turkish Foreign Ministry negotiated a "Shared Vision and Structured Dialogue" in July 2006 that pledged cooperation on regional and global challenges, and established regular bilateral meetings to reinforce that cooperation. The two countries also sought to collaborate in identifying secure sources of energy supplies for the Euro-Atlantic region. Turkey sees itself as a hub for the transfer of oil and natural gas from Central Asia to the West, while the United States, concerned about the growing dominance of Russian-controlled energy supplies, was eager to find new routes for pipelines.

Despite these efforts, U.S.-Turkey relations have continued to be problematic. Consideration by the U.S. House of Representatives of a resolution calling on the Turkish government to acknowledge the Armenian genocide caused extreme anxiety among Turkish policymakers. The fact that the Bush administration delayed mounting a strong effort against the resolution until after it passed the House Foreign Affairs Committee highlighted the lack of attention given to Turkish issues within the U.S. Government and the lack of a well-organized Turkish constituency in the United

States. Although a Turkey caucus exists on Capitol Hill, it cannot alone create broad-based support for the U.S.-Turkey partnership.

The most difficult issue between Washington and Ankara—one that many Turks see as a litmus test of the bilateral relationship—is that of eliminating PKK terrorist operations from northern Iraq into Turkey. Turks charge that the Kurdish region of northern Iraq (which has operated essentially autonomously since the mid-1990s) has become a haven for PKK terrorists and contend that the United States should ensure that its Kurdish allies in Iraq are not supporting terrorist attacks on Turkey and its citizens. The United States has repeatedly made clear that it accepts the need to stop PKK terrorism, and, accordingly, it appointed General Joseph Ralston as a special envoy to Turkey on the matter. Little progress was made, however, and Ralston resigned in mid-2007. Following a PKK attack in the fall of 2007 in southeastern Turkey that left 40 Turks dead, the Turkish parliament authorized military action into northern Iraq. Such action was aimed at destroying PKK bases and limiting PKK freedom of movement, especially its ability to cross the border. The U.S. administration sought to dissuade Turkey from taking such action, and has called on the regional government in northern Iraq to deal with the PKK but there have been no clear results. Instead, there have been reports of limited Turkish military actions in the border area, mainly air attacks, but now the precedent of a significant ground incursion has been established.

If the U.S.-Turkey relationship is to be put back on track, both parties must take concrete steps along the following lines:

- **The U.S. Government must address the PKK issue effectively.** It is often forgotten by Turks that the United States played a crucial role in apprehending Abdullah Ocalan, leader of the PKK, in 1999. However, that was 9 years ago, and the PKK has been rebuilding. The United States has told its Kurdish allies that tolerating havens on Iraqi soil for terrorist operations into Turkey is not acceptable. The United States must now push the Kurds to work with the Turkish government to stop further cross-border PKK operations. At the same time, the United States should encourage the Turkish government to begin a long-term process of reconciliation with those in the indigenous Kurdish community who have not engaged in terrorist acts. The presence of Kurdish legislators in the new Turkish parliament may provide a useful opening, although there are certainly questions about the relationship between their party, the Democratic Society Party (DTP), and the PKK.

- **Both the U.S. and Turkish governments must work to broaden support for the relationship in key constituencies.** Congress in particular needs to become more aware of Turkey's contributions as an ally, especially in Afghanistan, where it has made a continuous military contribution to the International Security Assistance Force-NATO, Afghanistan (ISAF), with significant military and civilian leadership roles. This might balance the desire of Congress to respond to its Armenian constituents. Over the long term, the solution will be Turkish-Armenian reconciliation, and the United States should do what it can to encourage such a development. A broader U.S.-Turkish civil dialogue is also required. Because the benefits of such efforts become apparent only after a significant time lapse, plans for such outreach should be developed very soon. In Turkey, the government must be clearer about not encouraging anti-American sentiments. It should not, of course, restrict freedom of expression, but it should be willing to provide a balanced perspective when the popular press and opinion shapers seem to embrace blatantly anti-American stories.

- **The bilateral economic relationship should be strengthened**. Until recently, there was little U.S. direct investment in Turkey. Since the 2001 economic crisis, Turkey has enjoyed significant economic growth, usually at a rate over 7 percent each year. It has now become the 13th largest economy in the world, and the seventh largest in Europe (Organization for Economic Cooperation and Development [OECD] 2006 and 2005 figures). The well-educated but inexpensive workforce and relatively open access to the EU market should make Turkey a good location for some U.S. companies. Some progress in this direction has already been made. In 2005, the United States was Turkey's fourth largest trading partner. In 2006, U.S. firms were responsible for about 20 percent of foreign direct investment (FDI) moving into Turkey, which increased dramatically in 2005 ($9.6 billion total) and 2006 ($17.2 billion) from previously low levels (U.S. Government statistics). Of course, governments have a limited role in encouraging economic ties, but both governments would find it helpful to have a larger business constituency with a stake in stronger and more stable U.S.-Turkish economic relations.

- **The United States should take a more proactive role in addressing the Cyprus issue.** Too many U.S. policymakers assume that since Cyprus is an EU member and Turkey a candidate, the Cyprus issue is now an internal EU matter. However, since Cypriot membership gives it a veto over even fairly small steps such as direct assistance to the Turkish Cypriot community, the EU is essentially impotent in this area. Instead, the United States must use its position on the United Nations (UN) Security Council to push for a settlement, based either on a revived Annan Plan or on another initiative by Secretary General Ban Ki Moon

Turkey in Europe?

Rebuilding the Turkey–U.S. relationship will be much easier if Turkey makes progress in its bid to become an EU member. Turkey must prove that it is able to implement the EU's *acquis communautaire*, the massive—and growing—body of EU laws and regulations on everything from environmental protection to social welfare and beyond. This is a tall order, and it will be 10-12 years before Turkey could reach that point. Some areas of law have caused concern, especially Turkish adherence to minority rights (e.g., as they affect the Kurdish population) and the continued existence of Turkish Article 301. Most Turks involved with the accession process realize that they have much left to do, but they also have confidence, along with their supporters in the EU, that they will achieve the *acquis* in a reasonable time.

The European debate over Turkish accession has raised some fundamental issues, however.[3] These are not about Turkey, but rather about what kind of

European Union will exist in the future. What will be the final borders of the EU? Is the EU a Christian region? Is it a place where all religions are openly practiced? Or is it a region with strict divisions between religion and public life? Some opponents of Turkish membership doubt whether Turks share basic "European values"; but what are those values, and how diverse and inclusive should they be in an expanding Union? The North Atlantic Treaty Organization (NATO) also expects its members to share certain values. Turkey is a long-time member of the Alliance. Is that an indicator of appropriate values? Finally, Europe already has a significant Muslim population, and by the time decisions must be made about Turkey in 10 years or so, that population will be even bigger. If Turkey's status as a Muslim country makes it impossible for Turkey to join the Union, what are the implications for the many Muslims who already live in the Union, or for other candidate countries such as Bosnia, Albania, and perhaps Kosovo?

Advocates of Turkish membership argue that bringing Turkey into Europe's body politic is strategically important; it will anchor Turkey in the West, and Turkey can be a vital bridge for Europe to the wider Middle East. The EU already feels the impact of the current conflicts in the broader Middle East, including increased terrorism and immigration. Europe is today very much involved through its role in the Quartet and the participation of European troops in Lebanon as part of the UN Interim Force in Lebanon (UNIFIL). The EU is likely to play an increasingly active role in the region, and having Turkey as a member would provide greatly enhanced strategic weight and regional credibility, according to this view. Others argue, however, that admitting Turkey, which borders on Iraq and Syria, would bring the issues associated with these two countries into immediate adjacency with European space much more quickly. For them, the preferred option is to keep Turkey out of the Union and let it serve as a buffer between Europe and the vexatious Middle East region.

The membership debate has contributed to a growing Turkish skepticism, if not disillusionment, concerning the EU. The percentage of Turks who believe EU membership will be a good thing has declined from 54 percent in 2006 to 40 percent in 2007. Turkish resentment toward the Union has been compounded by what many Turks regard as EU duplicity on the subject of Cyprus. The AKP shifted the traditional Turkish government position considerably (and risked alienating the powerful national security forces) in order to encourage the Turkish Cypriots to vote Yes on the Annan Plan referendum in 2004. When the Greek Cypriots voted No but were still permitted into the Union, the Turks saw no penalties for the Greek Cypriots in holding up a long-sought settlement. When the Greek Cypriots — now members of the EU — prevented the EU from allowing direct trade between the Turkish Cypriots and the rest of the EU, Turkish frustration and resentment grew even stronger.

One favorable note in Turkish-EU relations is the growth in economic ties. For many in Turkey, the primary motive in wanting to join the EU is to stabilize the Turkish economy and attract foreign investment. By any measure, that goal is already being realized. To gain candidate status, the AKP began to open the Turkish economy, and the results have been impressive. Since 2001, EU exports to Turkey have grown at an average annual rate of 20 percent, and the EU is now Turkey's largest trading partner. The EU accounts for approximately 80 percent of FDI in Turkey, with €5.6 billion in 2005 growing to €12 billion in 2006.

Improving the Turkey-EU relationship will not be easy, as neither the membership issue nor the Cyprus problem can be resolved in the short term. Given that approval of EU accession will not come for at least 10 years and that Turkey will then face the need for each member to ratify accession, the uncertainty about Turkey's EU prospects will continue to weigh on EU-Turkey relations. Despite this difficult environment, Turkey and the European Union can take some positive steps to improve their relationship in the near term.

- **As with the United States and Turkey, the relationship must be broadened and strengthened at the civil level.** There is already a huge Turkish diaspora in Germany, but that is not the case in many other European countries where Muslim immigrants tend to come from Algeria, Pakistan, and elsewhere. It is especially important that European parliamentary leaders—both on the national and European level—be engaged in the effort to make the public climate on this issue more hospitable, as they will eventually be key to ratification of the accession treaty. As with the United States, ties between the EU and Turkish business communities should be expanded. Given the strong growth in the EU-Turkey economic relationship, this should, without great difficulty, create a valuable constituency for improved relations and eventual accession.
- **Turkey must reinvigorate its progress towards meeting the EU *acquis communautaire*.** With the latest round of elections now over and the issue of the presidency resolved, the AKP

has a mandate to continue with its reform policies. Perhaps most importantly, it must take steps to amend Article 301, as the AKP administration has pledged. The United States can provide occasional discreet reminders to the EU of the strategic importance of eventual Turkish accession, but in the end Turkey will not be admitted unless the European Union is convinced that it can implement and enforce EU laws.

- **The membership rhetoric should be toned down, both in Turkey and the European Union**. When EU leaders baldly state that Turkey will never be a member or when Turkish politicians infer that the EU is being duplicitous, it does nothing but polarize public opinion and impede the process of building stronger EU-Turkey relations.

- **Resolving the Cyprus issue would be the single most important step the EU could take toward improving relations with Turkey**. Although the EU has generally shown itself unable to take bold steps if any one member state is strongly opposed, it must find some way to break the Greek Cypriot's current hold on this issue. If the EU is deadlocked, its members may have to use other institutions, such as the UN or Organization for Security Cooperation in Europe (OSCE) to move forward, but they should not allow the current situation to persist. The new Cypriot president has pledged to restart motibund reunification talks and to meet the leader of the breakaway Turkish Cypriots. The EU should give consideration to encouraging these initiatives.

Turkey against Itself?

The deterioration of U.S. and EU relations with Turkey has coincided with increasing polarization in Turkish domestic politics. Turkey is no stranger to domestic political crises, having endured three military coups (1960, 1971, and 1980) and the so-called "post-modernist coup" of 1997. While the era of military coups seems past, observers of Turkish politics are generally agreed that divisions within the country are wide and growing. They differ, however, over the nature of that polarization. Is the division between Turkey's traditional secular elite and an increasingly powerful Islam-rooted AKP? Or is it between those who seek to reform and modernize Turkish democracy and a mixture of nationalist forces that are increasingly resistant to the European impulse?

Since the AKP came to power in 2002, it has actively pursued a reform agenda designed to meet the criteria for EU accession. The AKP has also overseen a significant improvement in Turkey's economy, although unemployment is still high. But while the AKP leadership describes the party as comparable to the Christian Democratic Party of Germany, many of its critics fear "creeping Islamicization," and look to attempts to criminalize adultery and allow graduates of religious schools to attend university as efforts to overturn Turkey's traditional secularism. With a traditional secularist, Ahmet Necdet Sezer, as president, the AKP administration faced limits on its legislation and appointments. But when Foreign Minister Gul became a candidate for president, the general staff of the Turkish military—which regards itself as the protector of Turkey's Kemalist-style secular political system—twice issued veiled warnings about the threat his election might pose to that traditional order. Nevertheless, the AKP won the July 2007 election, demonstrating that many Turks did not believe its particular brand of political Islam was a threat to Turkish stability.

As the AKP was expanding its hold on government, the opposition was also experiencing a fundamental realignment. The main opposition party, the Republican People's Party, led by Deniz Baykal has struggled. Prior to the 2007 elections, few observers saw it as an effective alternative capable of displacing the Erdogan government, despite its success in mobilizing supporters for large demonstrations against the prospect of a Gul presidency. In the election, its portion of the popular vote rose very slightly, from 19.4 percent to 20.8, but its share of seats fell by 66 to 112.

The most significant electoral growth was experienced by the Nationalist Movement Party, which entered the parliament for the first time, crossing the 10 percent threshold with 14.3 percent and gaining 71 seats. This group is increasingly skeptical of Turkey's bid for EU membership, and is especially concerned that EU accession will require Turkey to forfeit control over its own national identity and policies. Unlike the traditional secularist parties, this group presented an alternative presidential candidate, Sabahattin Cakmakoglu, who stood against Gul in the August elections. This gesture was largely symbolic as there was no chance he would be elected, but it did indicate a willingness to offer active opposition.

In another notable political change, 18 Kurdish nationalists were elected to parliament after running as independents. Given the current tensions over PKK terrorism and the suspicions over the relationship between their party, the DTP, and the PKK, it is unclear whether they can provide effective political representation for Turkey's Kurdish citizens. The AKP also garnered significant support among the Kurdish minority in the recent elections, winning numerous constituencies in the southeast.

Although these political changes have strong domestic roots, they also have been prompted by tensions in Turkey's relations with the EU and the United States. As Turkey's efforts to align its laws with those of the EU begin to affect domestic law enforcement, economic regulations, and minority relations, there has been an increase in support for nationalist political parties that are skeptical of the EU process. Many in Turkey, including in the military, see the U.S. invasion of Iraq in 2003 as partly responsible for the reinvigoration of the PKK and for creating enormous potential instability on Turkey's borders. This view has added to the rise of nationalism in Turkey, as many in the political elite conclude that traditional friends, such as the United States and other NATO allies, no longer take Turkey's interests into account.

NATO: Collateral Damage or Touchstone?

The deterioration of Turkey's relations with the European Union and the United States has also had a negative impact on NATO. This has not been Turkey's intention; indeed, Turkey has long been an active and constructive member of the Alliance. Since joining NATO in 1952, Turkey has been one of the most active nations in terms of its military contributions, with significant participation in both Balkan missions and Afghanistan. Unlike many member nations, Turkey has met—and usually exceeded—Alliance targets for military spending. Turkey has one of the largest military forces in NATO, albeit one primarily configured for territorial defense (a necessity given the threat from PKK operations), rather than rapid deployment outside its borders.[4]

During the Cold War, Turkey provided a strong anchor for NATO in the West, while NATO addressed Turkey's security needs vis-à-vis its immediate neighbors. When the EU began to develop its Common Foreign and Security Policy, Turkey reached out to the EU's defense arm, the Western European Union, and negotiated arrangements that effectively gave Ankara a "seat at the table" when its security interests were involved. The emergence of the EU's European Security and Defense Policy after the 1998 St. Malo meeting disturbed this arrangement, at least in the view of the Turkish government. A potentially powerful security alliance was emerging in Europe, and Turkey, as a nonmember, had no way to ensure that it would avoid acting against Turkish interests.

Turkey responded to this shift by drawing closer to the EU, reinvigorating its membership bid and becoming a significant contributor to EU military operations. Turkey also insisted that cooperation between NATO and the EU should be authorized in a way that allowed a NATO member to block a consensus that might threaten its interests. Turkey's position has effectively stymied any NATO-EU discussions of such issues as Darfur, energy security, anti-terrorism, and other matters lacking immediate operational significance for the Alliance. Turkey's frustration with the EU over the Cyprus issue has determined it to maintain this NATO member veto, which the Turkish government sees as its only form of leverage. The U.S. Government has been reluctant to press Turkey to lift its block, given the other tensions in the relationship.

Clearly the way forward is to find a resolution to the Turk-Greek division of Cyprus. Until that happens, however, Turkey is likely to feel obligated to restrict discussions about NATO-EU cooperation. Yet the demand for such cooperation is growing, in Afghanistan and elsewhere. If NATO-EU cooperation does not become easier, NATO may find itself excluded from acting on many issues where cooperation with the EU is necessary, and in that case U.S.-European cooperation generally is likely to suffer.

Despite this difficulty, NATO still provides opportunities for reinforcing Turkey's importance to Europe and the United States, and for rebuilding those relations. NATO is now operating more than ever in Turkey's immediate neighborhood. And as NATO reaches out to the Balkans and beyond to Georgia, Turkey should be encouraged to take a leadership role in strengthening Alliance ties with these neighbors. Ankara can then ensure that such outreach takes due account of its interests, while also working closely with the United States in making NATO a stabilizing influence throughout the Black Sea and Caucasus region.

Building New Partnerships.

The U.S.-Turkey partnership must be rebuilt. A stronger partnership will relieve the isolation that leads Turkey to defend its interests so intently within NATO. A stronger partnership will also benefit the United States — Turkey, along with most of its neighborhood, is of vital importance to U.S. national security. In many ways, Turkey is now more important to the achievement of U.S. strategic objectives than it was during the

Cold War. Turkey could play an especially vital role in three areas: enhancing energy security; restraining Islamic radicalism and terrorism; and stabilizing the wider Middle East region.

Strengthening the Washington-Ankara link will require restoring trust in the EU-Turkey relationship. Because the Turkish leadership looks to the U.S. Government as an advocate for its European ambitions, the success of the U.S.-Turkish relationship will be judged in part by Turkey's progress toward joining Europe. Moreover, Europe has as much at stake as Turkey and the United States—if not more—in meeting the challenges of energy security, terrorism, and instability in the Middle East. A trilateral U.S.-EU-Turkey approach to these issues could be especially effective.

The Bush administration has taken a step toward restoring the U.S.-Turkey relationship by fostering Turkey's development as a transit hub for oil and natural gas. Turkey has long been an important conduit for oil shipments, primarily on tankers through the Bosphorus. The environmental consequences have already been severe, and an accident involving an oil or, in the future, liquefied natural gas (LNG) tanker, could be devastating. Moreover, the Bosphorus is already one of the busiest shipping lanes in the world, and there is little capacity, if any, for additional traffic. Thus, Turkish ambitions for becoming an even more important transit hub have focused on the construction of oil and gas pipelines.

There are several schemes for oil and gas pipelines, some of which are under construction and others only in the planning stages. The Blue Stream and South Caucasus gas pipelines opened in 2005 and 2006, respectively, while the Baku-Tbilisi-Ceylan (BTC) oil pipeline opened in 2005. Most planned and recent pipelines are designed to bring Russian oil and gas to Turkey across the Black Sea, or to deliver Caucasus oil and gas across Turkey (as would the Nabucco gas pipeline and BTC). In some cases, these pipelines could also deliver Iranian oil and gas through Turkey—a prospect causing the U.S. Government to hesitate in supporting these ventures. But as concern about the dominance of Russia in European oil and gas markets has grown, so has U.S. support for these other efforts, especially when they provide alternatives to Russian supplies.

Turkey's role as a transit hub for oil and natural gas is not simply of interest to the United States. The EU and its member states have an enormous stake in the growth and diversification of energy supplies in the region. Ever since the Russian government temporarily stopped the flow of gas to Ukraine in early 2006, EU leaders have made clear that diversifying supplies away from Russia is a priority (Russia currently provides approximately 25 percent of EU oil and gas supplies). Thus, the EU has great interest in Turkey's success in transporting oil and natural gas from its eastern borders to Europe. The United States, aside from its own interest in seeing more oil and gas reach the world market, also has an interest in relieving its European allies of their dependency on one source of supply.

Clearly this is an area in which the United States, Turkey, and the EU should be able to work together. They all have an interest in diversifying oil and gas supplies, especially while boosting the economies of the Caucasus and eastern Turkey. The business case for each pipeline must be strong enough to attract private investors, but the governments, especially if working together, can foster corporate partnerships and help reduce the level of risk. A strong trilateral partnership in this effort would increase U.S. and especially EU energy security, while also strengthening the U.S. and EU case for a stable and westward-leaning Turkey.

Trilateral cooperation in energy security is only a partial response to the need to rebuild the U.S.-EU-Turkish relationship. Two other issues stand out for their potential in strengthening trilateral cooperation: terrorism and the Middle East region. The United States, the EU, and Turkey share a very real interest in seeing a decline in terrorism, especially that based on radical Islam. They also share an interest in building a more stable Middle East, one whose politics are no longer dominated by the Israeli-Palestinian conflict or threatened by potential Iranian nuclear proliferation.

Terrorism as a Unifying Force.

The United States, EU, and Turkey each have a very different experience with terrorism, which is reflected in their policy responses. For the United States, a limited experience with domestic terrorism was suddenly overtaken by the catastrophic attacks of September 11, 2001, catapulting the issue of radical Islamist terrorism to the top of the national agenda. Although U.S. personnel abroad had been targeted before 2001 (and there had been a failed bombing of the World Trade Center), terrorism became a reality for most Americans with shocking suddenness. U.S. success in driving al-Qaeda's sponsors, the Taliban, out of power in Afghanistan and the U.S. administration's focus on fighting the "war on terrorism" overseas reflected a military and national security orientation in the U.S. response.

In Europe, long experience with different forms of national terrorism (the IRA, ETA, Bader Meinhoff, etc.) led to an emphasis on law enforcement as the primary response. Although Europe has suffered some significant terrorist attacks, it has experienced no level of mass casualties equivalent to that of the World Trade Center. The arrival of al-Qaeda in Europe has raised the stakes, however, with the London and Madrid bombings causing serious loss of life. Al-Qaeda's apparent success in recruiting European citizens to carry out terrorist attacks has caused considerable concern.

Following the 2001 attacks, many European governments sent troops to the U.S.-led war in Afghanistan and later supported NATO's role in that country. Nevertheless, most European political leaders reject the term "war on terror." Despite these different perspectives, the United States and EU member states have developed significant cooperation in intelligence and law enforcement aimed at fighting terrorism. They have also taken the lead at the UN and elsewhere in imposing financing restrictions and other measures that have been key in reducing state support for terrorist groups.

Turkey has suffered more casualties from terrorism than either the United States or the EU; Turkish government officials often cite a figure of 35,000 dead from PKK actions. Most terrorist acts within Turkey or against Turkish officials have been at the hands of nationalist groups such as the PKK or Armenians. In recent years, Turkey has suffered a few attacks by "religious terrorists," i.e., those motivated by fundamentalist conceptions of Islam, including al-Qaeda operatives. Given the strict traditional secularism of the Turkish government in a country that is more than 90 percent Muslim, it is surprising that Turkey has not been more of a target. Certainly most Turkish politicians and analysts believe that their country is on the front line in the battle against Islamic extremism.

Turkey has responded differently to these two distinctive types of terrorism. In dealing with "religious terrorism," the Turkish government has used its authority to limit the growth of radicalism and focused on the role of mosques. The Turkish government has long taken a role in training imams and overseen the content of weekly sermons. The government has also sought to avoid entering mosques when in pursuit of terrorists, and has generally kept its efforts within a law enforcement paradigm. In responding to the PKK, however, the government has employed a much more military-based strategy. Past government efforts to root out support for Kurdish separatist terrorists led to a civil war and military occupation of the southeastern region of the country, which is heavily dominated by the Kurdish minority. With PKK bases now established in northern Iraq, the Turkish military is massed on the border and poised to take further action against those camps if it becomes necessary.

To date, the perceived failure of the United States to take actions against the PKK in Iraq has been a major irritant in the Turkey-U.S. relationship. It is time for the United States to ensure that there is no safe haven for PKK terrorists in Iraq, and it should be prepared to press the regional government of northern Iraq to suppress or control the activities of the PKK on its territory. At the same time, the United States must also encourage the Turks and Kurds to embark on a process of reconciliation. Obviously, this is easier said than done. In any event, the U.S. Government should examine how U.S.-Turkish cooperation against radical

Islamic terrorism might be strengthened, whether through greater sharing of intelligence or enhanced cooperation between federal and Turkish police and investigative agencies generally. Turkey-EU efforts to cooperate against terrorism have been slightly more successful. Anti-terrorist financial rules have made it more difficult for the PKK to raise funds in Europe, but Turkish officials do not yet regard these measures as sufficient. There are other opportunities for Turkey-EU cooperation in this area, ranging from enhanced law enforcement and judicial cooperation to sharing "best practices" in encouraging mosques to be places of worship rather than political radicalization.

Working Together for a Stable Middle East.

The United States and the EU have long been active — both separately and together — in looking for solutions to the tensions of the wider Middle East region. Although U.S. and European views of the Israeli-Palestinian conflict are often very different, they have sought through the Quartet and other mechanisms to find steps toward a solution. Most recently, the EU and several member states were participants in the U.S.-sponsored Annapolis peace conference. The United States and the EU have also worked together to find a way to reduce Syrian influence in the Lebanese government.

Despite statements at U.S.-EU and G-8 summits to the contrary, transatlantic cooperation has been less obvious in pushing for political, economic, and social reform in the region, and there are some differences over the desirability of such a course, given the risks posed by Islamic extremists. While the United States and the EU have cooperated closely on the issue of

Iranian nuclear weaponization, they split into several different camps over the issues posed by Iraq. Despite U.S. and European efforts, however, the wider Middle East region has, if anything, become less stable and more conflict-prone in the last few years. The prospect of a significant U.S. reduction in troop strength in Iraq after the next U.S. presidential election adds another element of uncertainty and potential risk.

Turkey has taken its own approach toward its neighboring region.[5] During the Cold War, the Turkish government focused on the threat from the Soviet Union rather than any challenge from its Middle Eastern neighbors. This perspective was reinforced by the Kemalist tendency to emphasize connections with the West over the historical Ottoman ties to the Middle East. But the 1990-91 Iraq war led to economic hardship for many Turks with business ties in Iraq, convincing Turkish leaders that they should protect their own interests in the region rather than relying on the United States.

Since then, Ankara has reached out to build a wide network of relationships. For example, while maintaining its support for Israel, it has invited representatives of Hamas to Ankara for discussions and maintained correct relations with the Syrian government. Prior to the Annapolis meeting, both Israeli Foreign Minister Shimon Peres and Palestinian President Mahmoud Abbas visited Turkey and spoke before the parliament. Ankara has also maintained cooperative ties with Iran, as both have large Kurdish populations and are concerned about the potential spillover effects of an autonomous Kurdish state in northern Iraq. At the same time, however, Turkish government officials are concerned about Iranian nuclear weaponization, especially since Turkey is already within range of

Iranian missiles. Perhaps Turkey's biggest concern, however, is the power vacuum likely to develop if Iraq becomes embroiled in a civil war.

Turkey's increased activism in the region should not be interpreted as an alternative to cooperative ties with the United States and Europe in dealings with the Middle East, but rather as a diversification of its foreign policy approach. In fact, this expanding role puts Turkey in a better position for contributing to transatlantic efforts to stabilize the broader Middle East. The AKP in particular is well-placed to help more moderate political organizations in neighboring countries, such as Fatah, understand what is required to develop public support in a democratic environment. Turkey's wide range of regional contacts may also be useful in expanding the debate about the region and developing comprehensive approaches. And while Turkey has sometimes been regarded with suspicion in the region due to the hegemonic tendencies of its Ottoman heritage, it now has more credibility in the region than does the United States.

Given the assets that Turkey brings to the table — economic, diplomatic, and political — the United States and the EU should reach out to engage Ankara more fully in the region. Such an effort could be especially important once the Israeli-Palestinian process initiated at Annapolis is fully underway. Turkey has a huge interest in having a stable neighborhood. Accordingly, the Turkish foreign policy elite sees their country playing an increasing role, whether in cooperation with the U.S. and EU or not. Turkey may be lukewarm toward some of the American ambitions for change in the region, but it is not unlike the EU in that regard. Working with Turkey will help ensure that U.S., EU, and Turkish activities in the region are compatible. Although there are likely to be some disagreements, such cooperation will also strengthen the Turkish relationship with the United States and Europe. At the very least, it will demonstrate that the United States and the EU take Turkey seriously on an agenda of prime importance to this key ally.

New Partnerships for the Future?

The United States and the EU have already compiled an impressive record of cooperation in anti-terrorism and the Middle East peace process. They are not always unified in their views or actions, but they have established mechanisms — including the Policy Dialogue on Borders and Transport Security as well as the Quartet — that bring them together on a regular basis to identify joint steps forward. For the most part, Turkey has been outside this circle of cooperation. Given Turkey's large stake in both fighting terrorism and maintaining a stable Middle East region, supplementing the familiar U.S.-EU dialogue with trilateral U.S.-EU-Turkey discussions would be beneficial to all. Turkey would bring considerable assets to these discussions — from extensive experience in dealing with political Islam to a wealth of contacts throughout the Middle East. By using those assets and working together, Turkey, the United States, and the EU are more likely to be effective in making progress against terrorism and regional instability. Such cooperation will help foster an EU-Turkey relationship that is not totally dependent on the ups and downs of the accession process, and it may even teach some skeptics the value of working with Turkey.

Granted, U.S.-Turkey cooperation on these issues is likely to be difficult, as it will resurrect the very issues that have been so divisive in the recent past.

Despite those differences, however, Turkey and the United States share an overriding interest in fighting terrorism and reducing instability and conflict in the wider Middle East. By working together—and with the EU—to pursue their joint interests, Ankara and Washington can reinvigorate their relationship and reinforce a new post-Cold War basis for a sustainable U.S.-Turkey partnership.

ENDNOTES - CHAPTER 1

1. See "Cyprus Elects Communist President," *Washington Post*, February 25, 2008, p.A9. The new president, Demetris Christofias, has "pledged to restart moribund talks to reunify the island and immediately agreed to meet the leader of the breakaway Turkish Cypriots."

2. For insightful U.S. and Turkish perspectives on the bilateral relationship, see O. Faruk Loğoğlu, Chap. 2, "The State of U.S.-Turkey Relations: A Turkish Perspective"; and Ian O. Lesser, Chap. 3, "The State of U.S.-Turkish Relations: Moving Beyond Geopolitics," in the present anthology.

3. For one European perspective on Turkey's relationship with the EU as well as with NATO, see Michael Lake, Chap 4, "Turkey: Tilting from U.S. to EU?" This chapter also draws on a commentary made by German Minister of Parliament (MP) Claudia Roth.

4. For Turkish and U.S. perspectives on the NATO-EU relationship and Turkey, see W. Robert Pearson, Chap. 5, "Turkey and NATO: New Images and Old Questions"; and Sinan Ülgen, Chap. 8, "The Evolving EU, NATO, and Turkey Relationship."

5. For insightful U.S. and Turkish perspectives on Turkey's role in the Middle East, see F. Stephen Larrabee, Chap 6, "Turkey's New Middle East Activism"; and Gökhan Çetinsaya, Chap. 7, "The New Middle East, Turkey, and the Search for Regional Stability."

CHAPTER 2

THE STATE OF U.S.-TURKEY RELATIONS: A TURKISH PERSPECTIVE

O. Faruk Loğoğlu

Introduction.

Developing policy recommendations on the relationship between any two states requires first an understanding of the nature and characteristics of that relationship, as well as a sound appraisal of its current setting. The chances of making that relationship work are likely to be slim and mostly accidental unless there is a prior appreciation of its foundations and its capacity to adjust to changing conditions, as well as an understanding of whether the national interests and priorities of the sides coincide. Similarly, to chart its future, one must know where a relationship stands today and how it got there. Awareness of the constraints and the opportunities present in the relationship today is essential for realizing its potential at an optimum level tomorrow.

In the sections that follow, I first establish the main features of the relationship between Turkey and the United States, then look at the current state of that relationship, and finally propose specific steps and measures for its enhancement and sustenance in the future.

The Nature of Turkish-American Relations.

We should note at the outset that the U.S.-Turkey relationship is a special one. The two countries are formal allies in the North Atlantic Treaty Organization

29

(NATO), the only such alliance the United States has with a Muslim country. The soldiers of the two countries have waged wars together in defense of freedom in foreign lands. However, despite that core solidarity, their relationship has been beset from time to time by specific issues that have considerably undermined its energy and performance. For example, in the mid-1960s, the Cyprus issue, and in the early 1970s, the dispute over poppy cultivation in Turkey, sapped much of the relationship's strength. In the mid-1970s, following its military intervention in Cyprus, Turkey had to face a U.S. arms embargo.

The relationship between Turkey and the United States rests on a solid foundation in terms of common values and shared ideals. Commitment to and respect for democracy, the rule of law, human rights and freedom, economic prosperity, and national security bind the two nations strongly together. Both are dynamic societies that seek their golden age not in the past, but in the future. It is these shared values and attitudes that have kept the two countries close together, enabling the relationship to withstand the vicissitudes and tests of time.

In addition ot the serious disputes noted above, the relationship has survived other crises, including the 1962 missile deal in the wake of the Cuban crisis, the 1964 Lyndon Johnson letter, and the March 1, 2003, decision of the Turkish parliament refusing use of Turkish soil as a U.S. venue for invading Iraq. The Cuban crisis between the United States and the Union of Soviet Socialist Republics (USSR) was resolved through a deal behind Turkey's back, entailing the removal of Russian missiles from Cuba in exchange for the removal of U.S. missiles deployed in Turkey as a NATO country. The Turks were never consulted about the deal. When in 1964, Turkey threatened to intervene in Cyprus to help the Turkish Cypriots facing ethnic cleansing by the Greek Cypriots, U.S. President Johnson sent a letter to the Turkish prime minister, warning him that if the Soviet Union attacked Turkey to protect the Greek Cypriots, the United States and NATO allies might not—contrary to their obligations under the NATO Treaty—come to Turkey's defense. In 1974, when Turkey did indeed intervene in Cyprus, the United States imposed an arms embargo which took almost 2 years of effort to remove. However, the most severe blow to Turkish-American relations to date came in early 2003, when the Turkish Parliament failed to approve the entry of U.S. troops into northern Iraq from Turkey. All of these crises worked to the detriment of the relationship and resulted in loss of mutual confidence, requiring in turn much time and effort to repair.

The Turkish-American relationship is well-endowed and richly textured, but it does have a major weakness: the economic dimension is not strong enough. The amount of trade between the two countries is not nearly commensurate with the size of their economies. The number of American tourists visiting Turkey is small. U.S. investments in Turkey are still limited and investors hesitant. Turkish business executives, on the other hand, prefer markets more familiar and closer to home. Without a strong mutual economic stake in the relationship, it will remain fragile, ever vulnerable to the tensions and crises which normally arise in any close state-to-state association.

The relationship is asymmetric. Turkey is a regional power with outreach into several adjacent areas including the Balkans and Central Asia. Turkish interests, concerns, priorities, and timelines are primarily shaped by localized perceptions and are processed within a framework whose references are regional. Turkish regional concerns and perspectives are much more detailed and sophisticated in comparison to those of the United States, whose perceptions, being global, are manifested in broad strokes. The United States is a superpower whose interests and needs are calculated on a planetary scale, meaning it is generally not fine-tuned to the sensitivities of a regional actor like Turkey. Moreover, whereas Turkish foreign policy requirements change more slowly, U.S. concerns and priorities shift and evolve much more rapidly.

Thus, when U.S. views are communicated to the Turks, they do not always sit well with the Turkish mindset. For the United States, its requests are always important and of high priority. But because the relationship is asymmetrical, what is crucial and immediate for the Turkish side generally does not carry the same importance or urgency for the Americans. In short, U.S. demands and expectations from Turkey are presented as if they are sacrosanct while Turkish needs and priorities are treated by the United States as only one small voice in a chorus of importunate petitioners.

The Turkish-American relationship is a sensitive and fragile one. It is easily sidetracked by specific events or careless comments of political leaders and public officials on both sides, or by commentary in the news media or even the movies. When ill-nurtured and left to fend for itself, the relationship underperforms.

It is a relationship under permanent siege on the U.S. side. The Turkish-American connection faces constant attack by the hostile Armenian Diaspora and Greek and Greek-Cypriot lobbies. Their political and financial influence impedes freedom of action and clouds the judgment of American politicians and administrations in their dealings with Turkey, holding the relationship hostage to the interplay of domestic politics. Similarly, they affect the outlook of Turkish leaders toward Washington. U.S. decisions and actions, especially if they are linked to Turkish-Armenian or Turkish-Greek issues, are often—and generally with good reason—viewed by the Turkish political establishment with suspicion for being under the undue influence of Armenian and Greek lobbies. There is thus an element of chronic suspicion and distrust in the Turkish mindset about U.S. decisionmakers.

One other feature of the U.S.-Turkey connection is that it is slow in adjusting to change, both in the bilateral relationship as well as in the international setting. Foreign policy considerations underwent important changes in both countries in the post-Cold War setting, again in the aftermath of September 11, 2001 (9/11), and once again after the U.S. invasion of Iraq in 2003. The different rates of adjustment by the two sides to changing conditions have further exacerbated the problem, resulting in missed opportunities. The United States, with global concerns and other priorities, failed to put its weight behind a Cyprus settlement in the 1980s, gave only measured support to Turkey's fight against PKK terrorism in the late 1980s and the 1990s, and misjudged in 2003 what Turkey could deliver on Iraq. Turkey, on the other hand, mired in disputes with its neighbors and caught in the temporary euphoria of Turkic solidarity in those early days, missed the opportunity to develop a broad partnership with the United States in the Caucasus and Central Asia in the wake of the Soviet Union's collapse.

Since the end of the Cold War, Turkish-U.S. relations have witnessed a slow and subtle shift in their essentials. This shift entails a relative decrease in the importance of the military-defense-security or "hard power" dimension of the relationship and an increase in the importance of energy issues and matters of civilization, culture, religion, democracy, secularism, and gender equality, or "soft power" factors in the relationship. Turkey and the United States have not yet properly adjusted to this significant shift in their relations. Turkey wants to project its soft power assets, especially to the European Union (EU), while it still views its relationship with the United States more in terms of hard power needs and requirements. The United States, on the other hand, understands Turkey's true value as a democracy with a Muslim population in the context of the "clash of civilizations," but still relates to Turkey more in strategic and military terms.

The relationship is also constrained by the fact that while the national interests and foreign policy goals of the two nations on matters of mutual concern coincide and overlap, they are often not identical. Combined with the fact of common values, the convergence of national interests usually gives the relationship a strategic character that provides a suitable environment for close ties and cooperation. But to the extent that there are differences in those interests, real or perceived, they keep Turkey and the United States from cooperating productively.

The State of Turkish-American Relations.

The Turkish-American relationship is today in convalescence. Recovery is slowed by well-known make-or-break issues, especially surrounding the U.S. response to the PKK terrorist group and repeated resolutions by the U.S. Congress concerning Turkish-

Armenian relations. These ailments drain the relationship of its energy proper and keep it from branching out into areas where the two nations could productively work together. The relationship has also been badly sprained by the events over Iraq. Its recovery in the aftermath of the March 2003 decision of the Turkish parliament was better than expected, but it received further blows from U.S. failure to act against the PKK in Iraq. Incidents such as the detention of Turkish troops by U.S. forces in Süleymaniye during the initial phase of the Iraq war and the subsequent movie, "The Valley of the Wolves," did not help. Neither did certain public statements of leaders and officials of both sides.

Full recovery consequently looks like a rather distant prospect, in a context of persistently high anti-American sentiments in Turkish public opinion. Opposition to U.S. policies in Iraq is at its highest (more than 75 percent) in Turkey while support for the United States is at the lowest (under 10 percent). The outcomes of the presidential and general elections in Turkey in 2007 stiffened Turkish attitudes, official and otherwise, toward the United States (and the EU). If, in addition to failing to meet Turkish expectations regarding the PKK presence and activities in Iraq, Armenian resolutions reemerge in the U.S. Congress, the Turkish-American relationship is likely to suffer substantial damage. Coupled with diminishing Turkish support for EU membership and the proclivities of the Turkish Justice and Development Party (AKP) leadership, even the overall direction of Turkish foreign policy alignment might temporarily come under question.

The precise impact AKP's victory in the elections on Turkish-U.S. relations is not yet entirely clear. Prime Minister Erdoğan is trying to keep the atmospherics friendly. If he succeeds in demonstrating to the Turkish public that Washington is truly helping Turkey in its struggle against Partiya Karkeren Kurdistan (Kurdish Workers Party or PKK) terror and keeps the Armenian issue off the agenda of the U.S. Congress, then the Turkish-U.S. relationship could, in the short run, experience some sense of normalcy. But the texture of the Turkish-U.S. relationship is likely to weaken over the medium term for reasons related to internal developments in Turkey. The AKP can be expected to pursue an Islamist agenda more aggressively and with greater impunity than before. There are already ample signs of such a trend. Such a dynamic would be perceived and resisted adamantly by the pro-democracy forces and secularists as a threat to Turkish democracy and its underpinning, the principle of secularism.

An AKP majority in the parliament may not, therefore, necessarily translate into political stability if those members interpret their mandate as a license to enhance the role, place, and visibility of religion in state and society. The paramount goal for all concerned is the preservation and sustenance of both democracy and secularism in Turkey, because without secularism Turkish democracy will be gravely weakened. The choice for the United States could come to be between supporting a secular and democratic Turkey or watching Turkey steadily transform into a "moderate Islamic state."

Despite its cloudy state, the Turkish-U.S. relationship remains a strategic one because the two nations possess a substantial mutual capacity to collaborate on a wide spectrum of regional and transnational issues. Neither country is indispensable to the other, but both need each other in the current international setting and are poised to reap significant benefits if they can join their assets.

Guidelines and Policy Recommendations.

Repairing the relationship will take much hard work by both the United States and Turkey. They must both undertake the following first steps:

- To develop greater awareness of the current state of the relationship, both sides should seek a better understanding of the *nature* of the relationship, including its asymmetry and its sensitivities. They must work to identify what is truly important to the other side so that priorities are properly and realistically set and matched.
- Leaders and officials should affirm and underline at every appropriate opportunity the importance of the bonds between the two nations. They should consult each other before taking significant decisions of interest to the other side—a mere exchange of views is not enough. They must also be straightforward in identifying points of disagreement as well as of agreement. They should rely on official channels of communication, rather than communicating through the news media.
- Both sides should use the mechanisms identified in the July 5, 2006, "Shared Vision" document, signed by Foreign Minister Abdullah Gül and Secretary of State Condoleezza Rice. The two should engage in "expert level" and "policy planning" consultations and particularly encourage the "broad-based dialogue" called for in the document, designed to diversify the relationship through participation of civil society, business, news media, and the legislative

bodies of both sides. The annual "high level review" at the level of under secretaries and regular contacts at the political level should be held to make sure that the relationship is kept on track.

- To rebuild the military/defense relationship, a key element in the past, they should together review the state of defense/military relations in all its aspects, including improving weapons and equipment procurement procedures.
- They should try to enhance foreign policy cooperation, with special emphasis on the red button issues of our times, particularly terrorism.
- A special effort must be made to strengthen the economic dimension. This should entail, inter alia, fostering more trade, investment, and tourism, and also reviving the Qualified Industrial Zones initiative.
- The relationship urgently needs diversification. The United States and Turkey should encourage more exchange and cultural programs, with an emphasis on cooperation in the field of higher education and on civil society interaction. Cooperation in science and technology would especially benefit from the inclusion of the high profile community of Turkish American scientists and scholars in the United States. Finally, it would be useful to establish joint specialized bodies, including state and civil society components, for countering cultural and religious clashes and conflicts, and promoting harmony among civilizations.

In addition, the United States must move forward in the following ways:

- Most importantly, take credible and concrete steps to help end the PKK presence and activities in Iraq. In addition, Washington should restate its commitment to Iraq's territorial integrity and work to discourage Kurdish separatism in that country. It should encourage continued delay or cancellation of the Kirkuk referendum, given that Kirkuk is the centerpiece of the Iraqi Kurds' strategy to break away from Iraq.

- On regional issues, engage Turkey more actively in the Middle East Peace Process and particularly support Turkish-Israeli-Palestinian trilateral cooperative undertakings. Turkey and the United States should continue to exert joint efforts to promote democracy, the rule of law, and human rights in the Middle East and in Central Asia. At the same time, the United States must also allow elbow room to Turkey in its dealings with Iran and Syria. The United States should be clear and honest about its intentions regarding Iran and assure Turkey that if any military action is to be taken against Iran, there will be no requests made of Turkey to facilitate any such action.

- Resubmission of Armenian resolutions in the Congress should be discouraged. In contacts with Congress, the White House ought to be clear about its opposition to the adoption of any resolution supporting Armenian allegations of genocide and engage the Congress accordingly. In keeping with this imperative, the Congress must become better informed and educated about the Armenian issue. Members of Congress should be encouraged to visit Turkey for fact-finding and consultations. Without taking sides on the issue, the United States should insist on and help devise means for dialogue between Turkey and Armenia as well as between Turks and Armenians. To encourage this reconciliation, the United States should energize peacemaking efforts to settle the Nagorno Karabagh problem and make Turkey a more active partner.

- Avoid skepticism about the development of Turkish-Russian relations—the Turks know the limits. In fact, the United States should work with Turkey to help Georgia resolve its internal conflicts and its problems with Russia. The United States should also encourage the strengthening of ties between Turkey and Ukraine, a pivotal country in the European setting.
- Help and promote Turkey as an energy corridor and distribution terminal for oil and gas from the Caspian region, Central Asia, and the Middle East, and maintain support generally for the Turkish economy.
- Be more forthcoming on Cyprus by engaging the Turkish Cypriots and by urging an overall settlement through the good offices of the United Nations (UN) secretary general.
- Provide active and sustained support for Turkey's EU membership.
- Keep NATO strong; disallow any effort to undermine or supplant it.
- Support and promote Turkey's candidacy for UN Security Council membership in 2009.
- Avoid interfering or creating the impression of interference in Turkey's domestic politics.

Above all, avoid involvement in internal Turkish debates on matters of religion, religious sects, secularism, and nationalism, but instead take the general position that these are issues for Turkish democracy to handle.

Turkey must also work hard at reinforcing and strengthening the relationship. It should:

- Offer ideas and advice on regional issues of common concern. It should be especially proactive about its role in resolving regional conflicts in the Middle East, the Caucasus, and the Balkans. As the same time, it should be sure to coordinate the Turkish role more closely with U.S. efforts. It should not attempt or appear to mediate on behalf of the United States unless it is specifically requested to do so, but instead should act as a facilitator to enhance the quality of communication and understanding between the United States and its interlocutors in Turkey's various neighboring regions, particularly with regard to Iran and Syria.
- Work with the United States in forging closer ties between the Caucasus and Central Asian countries and the transatlantic community. This should include supporting joint programs and activities with the United States to bolster the defense structures of the Caucasus and Central Asian countries, including the establishment of closer relations with NATO.
- Encourage U.S. partnership in and contributions to the Black Sea region to foster security and prosperity in the area.
- Be a willing and consistent partner in energy matters and turn energy cooperation into a

vital and long-term connection between the two countries.
- Be a strong and steady voice in and for the transatlantic community.

CHAPTER 3

THE STATE OF U.S.-TURKISH RELATIONS:
MOVING BEYOND GEOPOLITICS

Ian O. Lesser

As Ambassador Marc Grossman has observed, the United States and Turkey are not natural allies. The countries are divided by distance, culture, and the natural differences in perspective between a global and a regional power. For Americans, the relationship has been sustained by broad-gauge geopolitical ideas, above all the notion of Turkey as a "bridge" between strategically significant regions, between the Muslim world and the West, and between north and south. In the Cold War context, Turkey was also seen as a strategic "barrier" to Soviet expansion, a role that some, especially in Europe, still see Ankara playing in relation to risks from the Middle East and Eurasia.

Until quite recently, Turkish strategists have held similar views about the importance of the United States as a global partner in the containment of regional adversaries, and as a backer of Ankara's strategic priorities, from European Union (EU) membership to energy projects. Turks have long balanced a desire for a seat at Washington's strategic table with deep-seated suspicion regarding U.S. intentions in Turkey's neighborhood (and toward Turkey itself). The Iraq war has greatly reinforced Turkish suspicion, and has led to a searching debate about U.S. power and its meaning for Turkey. Most recently, Turkey's political crisis—the Islamism vs. secularism debate—has reinforced Turkish sensitivities about U.S. preferences in Turkey.

This traditional and mutually reinforcing focus on

geopolitics as the backbone of cooperation has led to considerable volatility, frustration, and hollowness in the bilateral relationship.

The Myth of a Golden Age.

The current strategic environment, with immediate challenges in Iraq, Iran, and elsewhere in Turkey's neighborhood, places direct, practical demands on U.S.-Turkish relations — tests rarely encountered in past decades. It is too simple to contrast post-March 2003 frictions between Turkey and the United States with a previous "golden age" of cooperation. In reality, Turkish-U.S. relations since the 1960s have been characterized by recurring tensions, including widespread anti-Americanism, arms embargoes, and disagreements over the Aegean, Kurds, northern Iraq, and the Partiya Karkeren Kurdistan (Kurdish Workers Party or PKK). Few, if any, of the contentious issues on the bilateral agenda are truly new. Yet the relationship has endured because of shared interest in larger strategic "projects," from the containment of Soviet power to Turkey's EU candidacy.

Changing Bilateral Dynamics.

What is new, and gives today's troubled relations special meaning, is the substantially changed foreign and security policy outlook on both sides.
- On the Turkish side, the Justice and Development Party (AKP) government, and the social movement it represents, has spurred changes on the domestic scene. But it has also brought a new look to Turkey's foreign policy, with more attention to the north, east, and south. AKP strategists argue that this is simply useful

diversification and a search for "strategic depth." Others in Turkey and Washington are concerned that it suggests a more fundamental shift in Turkey's strategic orientation, fueled by increasing ambivalence about Turkey's European project and irritation with the United States. By design or by circumstance, more of Turkey's external policy energy is now devoted to relations with Russia, Iran, Syria *et al.*, and rather less to the maintenance of relations with Washington and Brussels. Does this add up to a shift in national orientation? Probably not. The weight of Turkish economic, political, and security interests still lies with the West. The Middle East is still seen more as an area of risk than a place of opportunity. And relations with Moscow still carry the burden of geopolitical competition and centuries of suspicion. Closer Turkish relations with Iran and Syria may complicate the bilateral relationship with the United States. But there may also be advantages for U.S. policy. It is noteworthy that when EU foreign policy chief Javier Solana held critical talks with his Iranian counterpart on the nuclear issue in April 2007, these talks were held in Ankara.

- Populist politics, vigorous news media, and a more diverse set of actors with international interests mean that public opinion now counts in Turkish foreign policymaking. Moreover, the public and elite mood has turned decidedly negative about the United States. This development, combined with the recurrent suspicion held by Turkey's foreign policy heavyweights — and the atmosphere of strident nationalism in almost all sectors of society — has made Ankara an increasingly difficult and sovereignty-conscious partner. Perceived rejection by Europe, renewed PKK violence, and a pervasive sense of national insecurity make nationalism the common denominator in much of contemporary Turkish politics. (Turkey is not alone here — a resurgent nationalism is observable elsewhere on the international scene.)

- On the U.S. side, the post-September 11, 2001 (9/11), focus on specific security challenges, with less attention to long-term regional alliances, has encouraged a tougher style in dealing with allies like Turkey, and tougher criteria for measuring cooperation. Key defense constituencies in the United States remain disenchanted with Turkey based on the March 2003 denial of a northern invasion theater against Iraq (even if much logistical support for the U.S. presence in Iraq still goes through Incirlik Airbase). The Iraq war has triggered a profound debate in Turkey, not just about the specifics of U.S. policy, but about the nature of U.S. power. More revolutionary, "transformational" strategies in the Middle East are a poor fit with Turkey's conservative, status quo approach to adjacent regions.

By contrast, Turkey's strong economic performance since the financial crisis of 2000-01 has spurred much stronger U.S. private sector interest in Turkey. Recent investments by Citibank (in Akbank) and GE Capital (in Garanti Bank) are leading examples. Turkey has led the Organization for Economic Cooperation and Development (OECD) in sustained growth over the last 5 years (6-7 percent per year), and the country has attracted more foreign direct investment (FDI) in the last 3 years than in the previous 80. Turkey now counts some 24 dollar billionaires, only slightly fewer than in Japan. The question, "Are we losing Turkey?" is fashionable in Washington, but not on Wall Street. Over time, this economic interest could produce a strong new constituency for U.S.-Turkish relations — if the current political instability does not lead to financial instability.

Beyond Geopolitics.

A reinvigorated U.S.-Turkish relationship will be less strictly bilateral, lower in expectations, less geopolitically preoccupied, but more focused on practical cooperation at the core. Some places to start:

- **Put Turkey at the center of regional diplomacy for Iraq**. The debate in the United States has focused on the role of Iran and Syria, but Turkey is rarely mentioned. Ankara has at least as much leverage over key aspects of the Iraq scene, and a leading stake. It is imperative that the United States convey a stronger interest in Turkey's concerns about the PKK and the future of northern Iraq. Coordinated action against the PKK should be at the top of the agenda. Turkey and the United States share a core interest in Iraqi stability. But if a more concerted approach is not forthcoming, there is a risk that Turkey will go it alone, as it has now shown strong signs of doing, with negative consequences for all sides. More emphasis should also be given to the very important logistical role Turkey has been playing in Iraq (perhaps 75 percent of materiel to support coalition operations in Iraq goes through Turkish ports and airports) — a reality that should weigh more heavily in congressional attitudes toward Turkey.

- **Focus on nuclear and missile proliferation as a long-term policy planning priority with Turkey**. The emergence of one or more new nuclear or nuclear-ready powers in the Middle East will have a profound effect on the strategic environment around Turkey. Turkey is unlikely to "go nuclear," but Ankara can be a key partner in containing and managing Iranian ambitions. NATO can be a useful voice to engage Turkey on this issue (this might also be true on the issue of the PKK and Iraq). Future U.S. and NATO missile defense umbrellas should certainly cover the most exposed members of the Alliance, including Turkey.

- **Foster a more diverse relationship**. Turkish and U.S. observers have long complained about the shortcomings of a relationship too heavily focused on security matters. The security relationship is likely to remain unpredictable in key respects, but the economic and other dimensions of the relationship, while expanding, remain underdeveloped (precisely the opposite of U.S.-India relations, for example). The economic aspect is closely related to Turkey's continued convergence with European practice in various sectors, whatever the prospects for EU membership per se.

- **Avoid the temptation to try to shape Turkish internal politics**. The current political crisis in Turkey has resulted in close scrutiny there of official U.S. attitudes toward democracy, civil-military relations, and the Islamism-secularism debate. U.S. policy should certainly favor democratic processes, but should also make clear that these are Turkish dilemmas, to be solved by Turks. U.S. leverage on the Turkish internal scene is limited, and it would be easy to "do harm" through an overly assertive approach to Turkish internal affairs.

- **Think about U.S.-Turkish relations in transatlantic terms**. In key areas, from engagement with Iran to attitudes toward the Palestinian-Israeli dispute, Turkish foreign policy is essentially in the European mainstream. This and other factors suggest that the prospects for a revived U.S.-Turkish strategic relationship depend critically on the restoration of transatlantic relations as a whole. A troubled transatlantic relationship will make a troubled relationship between Washington and Ankara much more difficult to fix, and will force Ankara into a series of uncomfortable foreign policy choices in the years ahead.

CHAPTER 4

TURKEY:
TILTING FROM U.S. TO EU?

Michael Lake

The simple approach to the Turkey-U.S.-European Union (EU) relationship has been to assume that as Turkey grows closer to the EU through the accession process, the relationship with the United States would assume less salience. This may well become the case in the fullness of time. For now, however, this idea of a tilt from the United States to the EU is too simplistic. Even if it eventually becomes a member state of the EU, Turkey will always continue to regard its relations with the United States as a fundamental pillar of its stability. Turkey historically feels threatened by several of its neighbors, including Russia. Stability is its number one priority and the number one responsibility of any government—except perhaps for getting itself reelected—so that Turkey will also want the best possible relationship with the United States.

A return to normality in that relationship is of the highest importance to the Turkish establishment, something diplomats realize is difficult to get across to the public during this time of malaise, if not crisis, in Turkey's relations with the EU, and the very bad Turkish public opinion polls regarding the United States. The big issues are general opposition to the campaign in Iraq; a feeling that the United States is doing little or nothing to curb the Partiya Karkeren Kurdistan (Kurdish Workers Party or PKK) in northern Iraq, which particularly agitates the Turkish military; and a sense of incomprehension and dismay that their hitherto strategic ally could contemplate passing a resolution in Congress which would effectively convict the old Ottoman regime of genocide of the Armenians in 1915, with the aim of punishing modern Turkey in order to please a foreign (Armenian) diaspora which has local votes in the United States.

The Turkish people have thus come to feel somewhat alienated from the United States and, to a lesser extent, from the EU. But the traditional elites know that a return to normality in relations with the United States is essential. A return to normality in U.S.-Turkey relations is also in the interests of the EU, which regards Turkey's stability as a prime asset. All relevant EU briefing papers refer to Turkey as an island of stability in a turbulent region.

Turkey regards the EU as the second pillar of its stability. Moreover, although the United States no longer regards Turkey as a strategic partner (which was its status throughout the Cold War and perhaps until 2003), the EU does indeed regard Turkey precisely as such a partner. Indeed, it has claimed Turkey as a strategic partner of European countries for nearly a century — for half of which time Turkey has been a member of the North Atlantic Treaty Organization (NATO) and a substantial European contributor of its sizable land forces as well as other important military assets. In particular, the EU regards the role Turkey is playing in the broader Middle East as a stabilizing one in the mutual interest. The EU appreciates the role Turkey indirectly plays in the European Security and Defence Policy (ESDP), its contributions of forces, aid, and sometimes support for refugees in Bosnia-Herzegovina, Kosovo, Macedonia, Lebanon, and the Congo, and, until recently, civil leadership of NATO forces in Afghanistan. EU ministers and commissioners tell the Turks that together they can help to dispel the alleged clash of civilizations.

It is instructive to note that during the captivity of 15 British naval and marine personnel in Iran in March-April 2006 the Turkish Prime Minister Recep Tayyip Erdogan telephoned the Iranian President Ahmedinejad seeking access for the Turkish ambassador in Tehran to visit the captives, and Foreign Minister Abdullah Gül spoke personally to Iranian Foreign Minister Manuchehr Mottaki when they met at an international conference.

How has Turkey's candidacy for EU membership affected its foreign policy? When Turkey was planning to join the EU customs union in 1995, Turkish officials pledged, in my presence, that if they got into the customs union they would closely follow the EU's common foreign and security policy. This has happened. This Turkish policy is also part of its accession (i.e., membership) program. Within this framework, the EU regards Turkey as having achieved an advanced level of alignment in external relations. In the United Nations, for example, Turkey is in line with the EU on 92 percent of issues and formal EU declarations.

In return, has Turkey's candidacy affected EU foreign policy? It has certainly clarified the EU's strategic view of Turkey. Apart from its status and qualities as a strategic partner, the EU sees Turkey as a major economic and social partner in the region. Turkey is now the seventh biggest trade partner of the EU, and the EU accounts for between 50 and 60 percent of Turkey's trade. EU investment in Turkey is growing by multiples of past annual percentage rates.

The EU takes very seriously two areas of interest in which Turkey plays a pivotal role. One is the security of the energy supply in an EU which includes Turkey, especially since Turkey would have on its borders the most energy-rich regions on the planet. Turkey is in the process of becoming a major energy hub providing access to energy independent of Russia, which has damaged its credibility as a reliable supplier.

The second area of interest is Turkey's impact on several transport modes, including its potential for new and greatly improved corridors for road, rail, air, and maritime pipeline connections between Europe and its southern neighborhood. This infrastructure, which would be heavily financed from EU "cohesion funds" after Turkey's accession to the EU, would facilitate the economic and trade integration of the Mediterranean region as a whole.

Probably the most dynamic factor influencing the current EU view of Turkey — apart from controversy created by those such as French leader Nicolas Sarkozy who has stated flatly that he wants to keep Turkey out of the EU — is the bigger and rather successful role it is playing in the Middle East. It has good, uniquely long-standing working relations not only with Israel and the Palestinians (both Prime Minister Ehud Olmert and a Hamas delegation have visited Turkey), but also with Saudi Arabia, whose King Abdullah paid a first ever visit to Turkey in 2007, with Iran (Prime Minister Tayyip Erdogan was there in 2007), and with Syria. Turkey's relations with Iran and Syria may not have pleased the United States, nor did the visit of Hamas to Turkey last year go down well, but it now seems that Turkey was ahead of the game. It is not Turkey that seems out of step.

President Hosni Mubarak of Egypt paid an official visit to Ankara in early 2007 along with a huge entourage, including four ministers. The leaders of these two so-called "invisible rivals" consented to a new "strategic dialogue" and signed a new agreement to improve bilateral relations between Egypt and Turkey, including gas, trade, and investment projects, with a special eye on an Arab gas pipeline expected to be built through Turkey by 2009-10. In March, the EU and Egypt adopted an EU-Egypt Action Plan under the European Neighbourhood Policy, setting an agenda for the next 3 to 5 years over a wide range of sectors, based on Egypt's own reform agenda in the economic, social, and political spheres. The European Neighbourhood Policy, a standing conditional offer to all neighboring countries from Belarus to Morocco, offers access to the EU's vast internal market in return for democratic and market reforms. Egypt is the eighth country to sign up for an Action Plan. Others include Ukraine, Israel, Jordan, the Palestinian Authority, Tunisia, and Morocco. Turkey does not qualify for the Neighborhood Policy because it is a candidate for membership in the EU.

Turkey has always maintained correct relations with Iran, and, setting aside the ebb and flow of migration patterns, there are usually about two million Iranians living in Turkey at any one time. Now Turkey and Iran have agreed to establish a "strategic alliance" in the energy sector, aiming at cooperation in drilling for oil and natural gas, natural gas power plants, and the transfer of Iranian oil and gas to Europe, which Europe needs. The United States has expressed concern about handing Iran such leverage.

The EU strongly backs Turkey's efforts in the Middle East, and has sought Turkey's support in persuading Syria to cooperate in resolving such issues as the assassination of the Lebanese premier. The EU has also sought Turkey's good offices in convincing Syria to follow policies that would facilitate Lebanon's participation in the European Neighbourhood Policy with its substantial advantages. Similarly, the EU has enlisted Turkey's help in persuading Iran to change its position on neighboring extremists and nuclear issues. Turkey fully supports the EU-3 efforts to turn back Iran's nuclear weapons ambitions. Both the EU and Turkey have now famously sat down with diplomats from both Iran and Syria.

If the United States and the EU are the first and second pillars of stability in Turkey, the region surrounding it comprises the third pillar of most concern. Turkey worries about the fragility of authority in several of its important neighbors, not least of which is Egypt. It is concerned above all with Islamic fundamentalism. Those in Europe who worry about Turkey should recognize that Turkey and its inchoate Muslim government regard fundamentalism and related terrorism not only as the great enemy of Turkey, but the enemy of all—the United States, the EU, and the Middle East.

How does the continuing Cyprus conflict affect Turkey's relations with the EU and within NATO? The answer is, "Pretty bad." Within the EU, Cyprus—that is, the Greek Cypriots—has the veto power to block the submission of any or all chapters of the *acquis communautaire* (the body of EU law) to negotiation. Although it has thus far refrained from doing so, it has already vetoed any action of the EU to open the ports and airports of northern Cyprus freely to EU traffic. In response, Turkey has politicized the issue of its contractual obligation to open its own ports and airports to Cyprus, the unintended effect of which in December 2006 was to block indefinitely eight chapters related to the customs union out of the total of 35 chapters.

Now, however, negotiations seem to have resumed on a more stable basis. The EU Council of Ministers has declared that the Cyprus issue should not be used as a precedent for blocking other chapters. It reached consensus in 2007 on so-called screening reports on six chapters of the EU's *acquis*, and two additional chapters were opened for negotiation under the German Presidency (an additional two were blocked by France).

At the other extreme, if the Greek Cypriots play an entirely negative game, they would try the patience of the other 26 member states, representing 470 million people, possibly beyond endurance. They could also provoke Turkey into walking away, in which case they would never get a settlement over land, houses, compensation, or authority in northern Cyprus, and thus lose the match. In the meantime Cyprus wants to be included in the EU-NATO "Berlin Plus" talks, to which Turkey objects on the ground that the dossiers are confidential, a view backed up by a December 2002 EU decision. Indeed, Turkey adheres to a parallel December 2002 North Atlantic Council decision excluding Cyprus and Malta from EU-NATO strategic cooperation. Cyprus is a big reason, if not the main reason, why there is no institutional relationship between the EU and NATO. Cyprus wants to join both NATO and the Organization for Economic Cooperation and Development (OECD) which gives Turkey a rare spoiling lever – one cannot be surprised that Turkey uses it.

The big issue, however, is Turkey's EU membership, and one day both the EU and Turkey will have to face up to the huge stakes involved, and to the question of whether Cyprus can continue to be allowed to bedevil a hugely desirable strategic outcome. The Cyprus question does not invite an easy answer. The disagreeable fact is that some EU member states are vaguely accused of hiding behind Cyprus in venting their own opposition to Turkey without making waves. But some strong supporters of Turkey, such as Britain and Spain, may yet call them to account.

The cost of the Cyprus problem to both sides is wholly disproportionate to the larger goal. Cyprus is in effect holding hostage the combined EU-Turkey destiny involving 550 million people on the basis of its insistence that Cyprus wins and Turkey loses. What has successfully driven the EU forward thus far, however, is a win-win dynamic for the EU vis-à-vis applicants. Cyprus is challenging the entire historic EU ethos over the issue of Turkey. Something eventually must give. Some of the more difficult challenges facing Turkey are likely never to be resolved until the Turks become more confident that they will eventually enter the Union and be compensated for their painful concessions. In terms of the EU maintaining a realistic prospect of membership for the Turks, the Cyprus issue casts permanent doubt. A noteworthy and possibly sanguine development is the pledge by the new Cyprus president, Demetris Christofias, "to restart moribund talks to reunify the island" and his expressed willingness "to meet the leader of the breakaway Turkish Cypriots."[1]

Nevertheless, we can expect continuing, robust work on the accession program. The European Commission delegation in Ankara is now the biggest in the world with 126 staff—larger than the traditionally biggest delegation in Washington—and, apart from monitoring the accession process, is managing more than €500 million a year in pre-accession funds to Turkey, which has also received €2 billion in loans from the European Investment Bank. These are large down payments by the EU on Turkish accession.

What steps could Turkey, the EU, and NATO take to strengthen Turkey's role in NATO and reduce differences between Turkey and the EU? Turkey regards its own role in NATO as being of great importance. Its role is secure and is a substantial asset to all partners. It is the only area where Turkey can score against Cyprus. The EU should be more careful about building up little so-called "battle groups," small groups of member states for specialized issues from which Turkey feels excluded.

Meanwhile, some more positive visibility of Turkey's history as a loyal and effective NATO partner would be useful. This history stands in stark contrast with that of France, which de Gaulle withdrew from NATO's military structure back in the mid-1960s and with that of Austria and Sweden, which both chose the path of strategically unaligned neutral countries. Turkey's current role as an active, contributing strategic partner of NATO and the EU should give the lie to the view of some European politicians that Turkey has no role in the EU.

The EU has approved a public information campaign aimed at the many elements of civic society —news media, academics, nongovernment organizations (NGOs), think tanks, trade unions, professional organizations, women's organizations, and so on—to foment widespread participation and dialogue between Turkish and EU societies so as to familiarize each side with the other. The European Commission will run the program with a budget of around €70 million a year, a lot of money in EU terms for a civic society project. My own sensing is that the number of truly productive conferences and seminars is rising.

What the United States can do to encourage Turkish accession to the EU is less clear and requires a certain finesse. The sad fact is that support from the Bush administration is often unwelcome, especially in the European Parliament, which now shares governance of the EU with the Council of Ministers. U.S. support for contentious EU projects is more likely than not to be counterproductive. Thus overt U.S. support for Turkish membership in the EU, however well-intentioned and justly based, is likely to make even more people apprehensive about the Turkish matter.

The best role for the United States in this area, therefore, is to help raise Turkey's visibility and portray it in a better light. In particular, it could highlight the many areas where Turkey's loyalty to NATO and the West, to western rights and obligations, provides continuing proven value. The United States could point to those strategic areas where Turkish participation is clear and helpful to an enduring common cause across the Atlantic. The public should come to its own more enlightened conclusions in the fullness of time, especially given that we still have another 8-10 years before an EU–Turkey Treaty of Accession lies on the table. Some may think such public enlightenment to be excessively optimistic, but it is possible if we concentrate on getting the ball over the goal line of EU accession, rather than allowing ourselves to be distracted by scattered events on the periphery. Moreover, it will happen not for the sake of the Turks, but because it is in Europe's best interests.

ENDNOTES - CHAPTER 4

1. "Cyprus Elects Communist President," *Washington Post,* February 25, 2008, p. A9.

CHAPTER 5

TURKEY AND NATO:
NEW IMAGES AND OLD QUESTIONS

W. Robert Pearson

Most people who follow the U.S. relationship with Turkey and the North Atlantic Treaty Organization (NATO) have focused on four widely shared perspectives together forming the conventional wisdom, if you will. These perspectives are, first, that the relationship has been good for both Turkey and NATO; second, that the U.S.-Turkey defense relationship is critical to good relations between Turkey and NATO; third, that for Turkey, NATO serves as a substitute for the European Union (EU) while Turkey awaits the outcome of its negotiations with the Union; and fourth, that the EU would like Turkey's soldiers in case of trouble and Turkey's economy in times of peace, but it doesn't want Turkey's Turks, to put it bluntly. There has been truth in all these assertions, but the picture today is more complicated, and the events to come are less foreseeable than at many other times. Today, the conventional wisdom as noted above need closer examination and more careful thought.

Turkey's relationship with NATO has changed constantly since 1952. Now, 55 years after Turkey was admitted to NATO and on the 50th anniversary of the EU, the question is how much energy remains in the relationship. To a certain extent, NATO still binds Turkey and Europe even without EU membership. Turkish officers and military personnel participate as equals in all of NATO's widely distributed commands, activities, and training facilities. NATO ensures that

Turkey participates in military and security structures in the Eurasian space with legitimacy. Article V, NATO's famously effective common defense clause, still ecompasses Turkey should any serious external threat arise, from Iran, for example. Turkey's membership in NATO also helps provide legitimacy for Europe's presences in central Asia, especially Afghanistan. The fact that Turkey assumed the International Security Assistance Force-NATO, Afghanistan (ISAF) regional command mission in Kabul twice is an excellent example of this link, as is the fact that Turkey also took over command of the Multinational Task Force South deployed in the southern region of Kosovo in May 2007. NATO also restrains Turkey's options. Memories of the Turkish occupation of northern Cyprus in 1974 must be a factor in any Turkish military consideration today about its options in northern Iraq vis-à-vis the Kurds (though such memories did not prevent the Turkish ground incursion in Northern Iraq in late February 2008).

As Turkey's domestic political scene evolves after the dramatic election of July 22, 2007, and the tensions between Turkey's military commanders and the elected government play out, NATO can be a highly visible emblem of Turkey's status and responsibility and a channel for reminding Americans and Turks together how critical it is in every circumstance to think hard before acting and to appreciate how much more valuable it is to work together. Here the United States has clear responsibilities which will be discussed later in the chapter.

For generations after the Korean War, Americans spoke with great pride and gratitude of Turkish sacrifices and victories in that conflict. This memory came to personify for many Americans the entire relationship. For Turks, Korea was important, but it never entered the Turkish consciousness the way it did for Americans. In the context of the Cold War, two American misconceptions arose from this experience and played an important part in shaping Turkey-NATO and Turkey-U.S. relations for decades.

The first misconception was the over-weighted U.S. focus on Turkey as a bulwark against the Soviets, to the detriment of other goals. Aiding Turkey's fledgling democracy, strengthening democratic parties in Turkey, seriously attempting to persuade Turkey to stop its runaway inflation, all were secondary goals compared to the need for Turkey's strong political will to face off against the Russians and to act as a forward platform for U.S. weaponry and intelligence during years of grave threat from the Soviets. The second misconception, which every Turkish leader heard again and again from 1952 on, was that Turkey was a uniquely important piece of geostrategic real estate. The lesson, in short, was that Turkey was important just for being Turkey, and that the United States did not ask more or need more from Turkey in the way of support.

However, from the U.S. perspective, Turkey's cooperation and steadfastness during the Korean and NATO experience did give rise to the belief that the Americans could ask the Turks for help — and expect it — without having to pay, promise, or commit too much in return. On the positive side, the good will earned by the Turks created a foundation of solid support in the U.S. military, on the Hill, and among the American people that persisted for decades. I am not recalling these events to be critical of either country, but simply to observe how the current of history, once established in a deeply etched channel, continues in the prescribed direction until other decisive events change its course.

From the 1960s through the end of the Cold War, there were a number of dramatic formative events. There were military coups in Turkey in 1960, 1971, and 1980. In each case, the fabric of democracy in Turkey was weakened, but the coups ultimately earned the support of the Turkish people by restoring order to the country. Moreover, the Turkish army, unlike so many others around the globe, each time returned power to the civilian leadership. In each case, its membership in NATO allowed Turkey to maintain dialogue with Europe and the United States and to preserve a form of legitimacy.

As a result of the Turkish invasion of Cyprus in 1974, NATO-Turkey relations plunged to perhaps an all-time low. Turkey felt betrayed by allies, who would not prevent the disaster threatening the Turkish population on the island, and the allies knew after the worst was over that the crisis would damage relations with Turkey for years. The recovery of Turkey during the years of Turgut Ozal (1983-93) also meant the restoration of good relations with most of the NATO allies, including the United States. During his 10 years in power, first as prime minister and then as president, Ozal reignited the Turkish economy and recouped the former warm U.S.-Turkish relations.

In 1996, Turkey and Israel signed a major military agreement. This opening has been severely strained at times, but despite improving ties with Syria, Hamas, and Iran, Turkey has never closed the door with Tel Aviv and values its role as one possible mediator in the Arab-Israel conflict. These events shaped, strained, and modified the essential course of the NATO-Turkey relationship, but they did not fundamentally shift it. There can be no doubt that the existence of NATO, even when not engaged directly, made it immeasurably easier to handle the difficulties and opened new opportunities to move ahead.

Then came a great seismic event—the collapse of the Soviet Union and the end of the Cold War—for which no one was really prepared. Neither was the Turkey-U.S.-NATO relationship prepared for the end of the Cold War. It was as if Turkey and NATO had been waltzing through history without constraints of time and space, when suddenly the band stopped playing, the musicians packed up, and the lights were turned off. Up until then, Turkey had been a favored dance partner, but suddenly there were a lot of other dancers from eastern and central Europe, some perhaps even more attractive. Turkey must have wondered in 1991 why it suddenly found itself standing on the dance floor all alone without even an escort to the new Europe. From that moment, Turkey and the United States began moving on different tracks, even if no one in the two countries saw it clearly at the time.

From 1991 on, Turkey's traditional military and defense industry allies in the United States continued to think about Turkey in the old ways. In fact, the first Gulf War, which effectively coincided with the final collapse of the Soviet Union, seemed to strengthen the view that Turkey was still the loyal ally, the staunch friend, and an attractive market for defense companies. However, the underlying structure was shifting. Though the pro-Turkey allies were still there, the external political and strategic geography had changed.

Importantly, in Washington there was a failure to grasp the danger flowing from the deep sense of disappointment in Turkey that emerged when the first Gulf War did not deliver on the promises made by the Turkish and U.S. leadership that Turkey would greatly benefit economically from the war. The Turks also hoped for an economic resurgence after the Cold War, a peace dividend, just as did the populations of every other NATO member. After all, the Turks had shouldered one of the most important responsibilities for NATO during the Cold War, facing off against Moscow. But the Gulf War intervened. Instead of the envisioned riches to flow from a new Iraq to Turkey, Ankara saw lost opportunities and a failure by the United States to make good on promised aid. The United States pledged billions in aid to Turkey during the first Gulf War, and none of this, or little of it, was ever forthcoming. Rather than benefiting from that first war, the Turks suffered the loss of key markets in the lower Middle East and their traditional business investment in the north of Iraq. In conversations in the late 1990s, the Turks would describe their losses as ranging variously from $35 billion to $150 billion. In short, the Turks thought the United States reneged on its pledges in the first Gulf War. The seeds sown by this disappointment lay dormant for a decade and then erupted into full bloom during the negotiations in 2002 and 2003 over Turkey's possible involvement in operations against Iraq. In 2002, few Americans recalled that the Turkish general staff had resigned in the face of Ozal's pledge to join the Americans in 1990, and no U.S. official acknowledged to the Turks the American failure to follow through with compensation as promised in 1990. But no Turk ever forgot his or her belief that the first Gulf War was generally injurious to Turkey and to its economy.

Through the 1990s, there was still a body of support in Congress for Turkey the democracy, but it seemed more abstract now. The Cold War rationale which had made the support second nature was no longer there. Before the end of the Cold War, of all the NATO states Turkey's democracy had penetrated the farthest east, where it stood in splendid isolation. This sense of singularity about Turkey now began to end. There were many new states east of old NATO now seeking membership. The states of the now-dead Warsaw Pact and of the former Soviet Union surged to the barricades demanding democratic governments and membership tracks for admission to NATO. They and the EU became the new darlings of political attention.

At the same time, the Turkish initiative to reach out to embrace the states of central Asia did not achieve its objectives. Upon achieving independence, the Turkic-speaking states first wanted to identify with the United States, Europe, and their institutions in order to obtain Western political backing, investment, and development funds. Still rebuilding its own economy, Turkey was not able to either provide sufficient influence with the West or muster the funds that the central Asian states desired. There was also cultural resistance. The Turks assumed they would be welcomed as benevolent kinsmen, but the governments of central Asia were not looking for a big brother. While the initiative was moderately successful up to 1994 and blunted some Iranian influence, it did not become part of a new political or economic grouping as Ankara had originally conceived.

The new post-Cold War security arrangements in the greater Middle East did not come through NATO. Victorious in the Cold War, the United States took up the great power game, now free to use ad hoc coalitions, backed by the United Nations (UN) and NATO where possible, but no longer relying on the veneer of external international legitimacy as much as it did during the Cold War. Turkey still preferred the security and certainty of international institutions and international legitimacy. As a diplomatically and militarily cautious state in 1990, Turkey protected itself militarily within secure borders in a dangerous neighborhood and diplomatically on the international stage through association with the consensus decisions of its allies. American discussions in the early and mid-1990s about the roles and responsibilities of a new empire would have raised questions in the Turkish mind about ultimate U.S. intentions concerning the region.

As a result, when no-fly zones were set up in northern and southern Iraq in 1991, the Turks and the Americans had different objectives. This was not a NATO arrangement, but a more loosely organized UN structure, and the participating coalition was smaller. Many in the United States saw these arrangements as a permanent noose around Saddam Hussein's throat and even a measure that might precipitate his overthrow. For their part, however, the Turks were happy for the stability that Saddam's authoritarian regime provided, particularly an end to the refugee flow, and they were largely content with his rule and its implicit certainty that Iraq would not collapse or splinter into ethnic or sectarian slices that could threaten its own stability (read an autonomous Kurdish state).

The desire to stay within clear international authority resurfaced after September 11, 2001 (9/11). Turkey was guided by the UN resolution immediately following the New York City and Pentagon attacks and actually tried without success to use that resolution to generate interest in a global definition of terrorism. Concerning Afghanistan, the NATO decision invoking Article V in favor of the United States gave Turkey unimpeachable authority to say Yes to the U.S. request for assistance in Afghanistan. In fact, in 2001 the

Turkish government gave its formal consent within an hour of the U.S. request for access to air space and bases for operations in Afghanistan. Turkey's secular leadership in 2001 harbored great antipathy towards the Taliban, seeing Kabul as a center of radical Islam that could ultimately threaten the social and political fabric of Turkey itself.

With continuing international legitimacy through the UN and NATO, Turkey acted very positively in Afghanistan, supplying forces and then a commander for the coalition forces there on two occasions. Finally a distinguished former Turkish foreign minister, Hikmet Cetin, served as NATO's senior civilian representative in Afghanistan during the important early years. By extension, Turkey answered a call from the UN following last summer's resolution and dispatched a number of troops to Lebanon. Turkey thus has demonstrated at regular intervals that it is clearly prepared to play a responsible role in crises within its region, including the participation of its military forces. In that way, Ankara has acted both to promote the role of key international peacekeeping institutions in the area and to fill a leadership role when Turkey's interests justify such action.

By contrast—even sharp contrast—with respect to the Iraq war, there was neither a UN nor a NATO mandate that provided Turkey even a fig leaf for its lack of equivalent authority under international law to agree to the U.S. requests for support. Ironically, the NATO decision on Afghanistan in October 2001 may have indeed been construed by some Turkish decisionmakers thereafter as the only correct (and safe) way for the country to proceed when deciding whether to deploy troops outside its borders or help another country invade a neighboring state (hence Turkey's reluctance to become the theater for a U.S. invasion of Iraq from the north).

Nor did the personal relationships forged at NATO prove to be especially useful to the United States. Retired senior Turkish diplomats, newly minted as fledgling politicians in Turkey's opposition party following the elections of November 2002, were in the forefront of those opposed to the U.S. request. Their motivations seemed to have been twofold. First, whatever the short-term cost to U.S.-Turkey relations, they wanted to damage the newly elected Justice and Development Party (AKP). Second, these men reported that because of their long diplomatic experience, they were the truly expert negotiators with the United States and would have secured a "better deal" for Turkey. Moreover, the actual military-to-military negotiations for possible cooperation between Turkey and the United States, as well as misunderstandings that occurred during the Iraq operation itself, left bruised feelings in both militaries.

Today, NATO's significance for Turkey continues to evolve. NATO itself has shifted from being an all-embracing alliance against a known threat to a forum for multilateral decisionmaking on security questions affecting the Eurasian land mass and, perhaps one day, even the Middle East. NATO, along with the UN, is a legal authority for the deployment of forces outside Turkey's borders, and only an overriding national interest is likely to change that approach. There are limits to Turkish commitment to international decisionmaking, but the record reveals that those exceptions are rare. Turkey continues to parley with its European partners within NATO, for example, to expand its opportunities to participate in EU military activities. NATO as a bulwark, both in its political dimension and in its multilayered and complicated military activities, still provides Turkey and the other allies a forum for patient, professional dialogue on sensitive issues.

However, NATO no longer serves as a status substitute for the EU. The EU option can be pursued only in Brussels. Turkey's NATO membership is no longer a cogent argument in Brussels for Turkey's EU aspirations. Especially since the elections of July 2007, Turkey is likely to be judged on its pace of further democratic progress. The Turks certainly do not see NATO as a substitute for the EU benefits. Turkey long ago realized that its future requires genuine economic growth, and only the EU can provide a satisfactory framework and discipline for these goals. So far as political reform is concerned, NATO as an institution historically did not generate momentum in Turkey on such issues.

Where do these trends lead Turkey, the United States, and NATO? First, Turkey will now pursue increasingly separate approaches in its dealings with NATO and the EU. While Turkey will remain a vital member of the Alliance, as a result of the Iraq War public support for NATO in Turkey may wane, perhaps never regaining the levels of the Cold War. Moreover, there has been for many years an ultra-nationalist (albeit minority) line of thinking in Turkey that has argued against treaty obligations with the United States or any other power on the grounds that such ties weaken Turkey's sovereignty. These views surface periodically in calls, for example, for Ankara to develop a balance of power approach and create stronger ties with Iran, Russia, central Asia, or selected Middle East states. These proposals may surface again over disappointment that NATO has done little to help Turkey in its fight against the Partiya Karkeren Kurdistan (Kurdish Workers Party or PKK) terrorism. In addition, given the great unpopularity of the United States in Turkey today, there is a risk that these calls will be accorded greater credibility in public debate.

A second trend might emerge from events in the former Yugoslavia and Afghanistan. As we saw earlier, following the Cold War, Turkey's importance within NATO changed. Today, however, that change provides a new opportunity for more Turkish activism, one that had been obscured before. From 1991 onward, Turkey's value to the Alliance became more and more a function of the political decisions it took with respect to the region and the military decisions it took supporting NATO's out-of-area ventures. This occurred first in Turkey's decision to join actively in NATO efforts in the former Yugoslavia, and, nearly a decade later, in its decision to join the NATO effort in Afghanistan. If Turkey continues this approach, the mutual importance of NATO and Ankara for each other could grow.

There is scope for the Turkish leadership regionally that would be very beneficial. The reelected AKP government could even expand its opportunities for dealing with a dubious Turkish military by politically associating itself more openly with NATO and helping to shape NATO's evolving doctrine concerning out-of-area operations. The future of the Black Sea region, with its mix of new NATO members (Romania, Bulgaria), key NATO partnership states (Ukraine, Georgia), a resurgent Russia, and nearby neighbors in conflict (Armenia, Azerbaijan), will present major policy challenges for Turkey in the years ahead. With a more active diplomacy and coordination within NATO, Turkey might provide a pivotal influence on both political and military issues.

For the United States dealing with Turkey within NATO, the Alliance framework also presents opportunities. The Supreme Allied Commanders Europe (SACEUR) have always maintained a positive relationship with the Turkish military and will certainly continue to seek out more occasions to keep Turkey engaged. NATO can serve as a vehicle for a healing process between the two militaries and for broader dialogue on regional issues within a shared framework of legitimacy as discussed just above. From the U.S. political perspective at NATO, more active listening is always a good thing.

While U.S. rhetoric praising Turkey has increased, concrete action by the United States against the PKK seems far too conditioned by the views of the Kurdish leadership in northern Iraq. The current situation harms both the United States and Turkey by allowing tensions to fester between Ankara and Baghdad over northern Iraq and by giving the PKK hope of driving a wedge between Ankara and Washington. Moreover, a Kurdish leadership in Iraq so in need of continued U.S. help for the future of its region should recognize its own interests in assisting Washington resolve the PKK issue. It is certainly in the long-term interest of the Kurds for the United States to have good relations with Ankara. A policy that relies on Turkish forbearance in the face of severe provocations leaves both timing and choice concerning northern Iraq in Ankara's frustrated hands, as we have recently seen. Washington cannot restore close ties with Turkey until the PKK issue is on the road to resolution. In this circumstance, one has to wonder why the United States permits this injurious scenario to continue. Only the United States can compel effective measures in Iraq. The puzzlement is that even with anti-American sentiment at an historic high in Turkey, Washington still procrastinates.

If the United States were at last to take visible steps to respond to Turkey's concerns, there would be a triple benefit. U.S.-Turkey relations would improve, Turkey's government would be able to begin to improve NATO's image domestically (which has suffered in Turkish eyes for a failure to be responsive to Turkey's terrorism threat), and Turkey would have greater maneuvering room to take the necessary political, economic, and social measures to improve the quality of life for its largely Kurdish population in the country's southeast. While NATO may not play a high-profile role, it can provide a setting for discussion of these issues away from both Washington and Ankara and thus play an indispensable part in achieving a necessary reconciliation.

In sum, Turkey is in a new relationship with NATO, and there are important opportunities for Ankara and for the United States in the current environment. There is an opportunity for Turkey and the United States to better use NATO's framework and avenues of communication to improve relations between their militaries and to help secure the political commitments necessary to put U.S.-Turkey relations on a better footing. U.S.-Turkey relations today are weaker than at any time since the Cyprus crisis of 1974. NATO can play a part in restoring those ties — the question is whether the parties will recognize and take advantage of the opportunities while there is time.

CHAPTER 6

TURKEY'S NEW MIDDLE EAST ACTIVISM

F. Stephen Larrabee

The last decade has witnessed a remarkable burst of Turkish activism in the Middle East. After decades of passivity and indifference, Turkey is emerging as an important diplomatic actor in that region. This new activism and independence represent an important departure in recent Turkish foreign policy. Except for a brief period in the 1950s, Turkish foreign policy has been characterized by caution and aloofness from deep involvement in Middle East affairs. For most of the postwar period, the Middle East was largely off limits for Turkish foreign policy.

However, this new activism in the Middle East does not mean that Turkey is about to turn its back on the West. Turkey is reintegrating into a region of which it has historically been an important part. The Republican period—with its strong rejection of involvement in Middle Eastern affairs—was an anomaly in Turkish history. For many centuries, especially under the Ottomans, Turkey was an integral part of the Middle East and the dominant power in the region. Turkey's current activism in the Middle East represents a reversal of that anomaly and a return to more traditional patterns of Turkish behavior.[1]

The Impact of the Gulf War.

The Gulf War was an important catalyst for Turkey's return to the Middle East. President Turgut Özal's support for the United States in the Gulf War represented a major break with Turkey's previous disposition toward noninvolvement in the Middle East. Özal saw the war as an opportunity to demonstrate Turkey's continued strategic importance and cement closer defense ties with the United States. Against the advice of many of his advisors — and the Turkish military — Özal threw Turkey's full support behind the U.S. military campaign to drive Iraq out of Kuwait. Ankara cut off Iraq's oil exports through Turkish pipelines as part of United Nations (UN) sanctions imposed on Iraq. It also deployed 100,000 troops along the Turkish-Iraqi border and allowed the United States to fly sorties against Iraq out of Turkish bases.

Özal hoped that his firm support for the U.S. military campaign against Iraq would bring important foreign policy dividends in terms of strengthening the "strategic partnership" with the United States and enhancing Turkey's prospects for achieving membership in the European Community (as the European Union (EU) was then called). However, Özal's hopes proved illusory. The strategic partnership with the United States remained a chimera while Özal's support of the United States did little to advance Turkey's membership in the European Community. Economically, moreover, Turkey paid a high price for its support of the U.S. military campaign in terms of lost pipeline fees and trade.[2]

As a result of the Gulf War, Turkey found itself drawn more deeply into the vortex of Middle East politics. The war marked a major escalation of Turkey's Kurdish problem. The establishment of a de facto Kurdish state in Northern Iraq under western protection gave new impetus to Kurdish nationalism and provided a logistical base for attacks on Turkish territory by Kurdish separatists in the Partiya Karkeren

Kurdistan Workers Party (Kurdish Workers Party or PKK). While many Americans regard the Gulf War as the heyday of U.S.-Turkish cooperation, for many Turks, as Ian Lesser has noted, the Gulf War is "the place where the trouble started."[3]

Iraq and the Kurdish Challenge.

The U.S. invasion of Iraq has also been a major catalyst for Turkey's new focus on the Middle East. Turkish policymakers had strong reservations about the U.S. invasion from the outset. While they had no love for Saddam Hussein, Turkish leaders saw him as assuring stability on their southern border. They feared that his removal would lead to the fragmentation of Iraq, strengthen Kurdish aspirations for an independent Kurdish state, and reinforce separatist pressures among Turkey's own Kurdish population.

Since then, Turkey has seen its worst fears realized. Iraq remains politically fragile and has become a breeding ground for international terrorism. Iran's influence has increased in Iraq and the region more broadly. And the Kurdish drive for autonomy — as well as eventual independence — has been given greater impetus. Turkey is now confronted with a very real prospect that an independent Kurdish state may eventually emerge on its southern border. Turkish officials fear that this could exacerbate separatist pressures among Turkey's own Kurdish population and pose a threat to Turkey's territorial integrity.

In the last several years, Turkey has witnessed an upsurge of violence by Kurdish separatists led by the PKK. The PKK has waged a highly destructive guerrilla war in southeastern Turkey resulting in the death of more than 35,000 Turks and Kurds since 1984. After the capture of PKK leader Abdullah Öcalan in 1999, the PKK declared a unilateral ceasefire. However, it took up arms again in June 2004 and has launched repeated attacks on Turkish territory from sanctuaries in the Kandil Mountains in northern Iraq. These attacks have resulted in the deaths of over 200 members of Turkish security forces since January 2006.

The Erdogan government has repeatedly requested U.S. military assistance to help eliminate PKK training camps in northern Iraq. However, Washington has been reluctant to take military action against the PKK because it cannot spare the troops, which are needed to combat the insurgency elsewhere in Iraq. In addition, military action against the PKK could destabilize northern Iraq, which is relatively calm compared to the rest of Iraq. The Kurds have been the staunchest backers of U.S. policy in Iraq. Without their support, any hope for the emergence of a unified and stable Iraq could collapse.

The reluctance of the United States to help Turkey militarily to eliminate the terrorist threat posed by the PKK has led to growing frustration and bitterness in Ankara, which repeatedly threatened to take unilateral action to eradicate the PKK threat and in late February 2008 did indeed launch a substantial week-long ground incursion against PKK targets in northern Iraq. The U.S. reluctance has contributed to a dangerous growth of anti-American sentiment in Turkey. According to a poll by the German Marshall Fund, among European nations, Turkey reports the lowest approval rating for President Bush's handling of international policies, with only 7 percent approving and 81 percent disapproving. The strongest negative feelings toward U.S. leadership were also found in Turkey, where 56 percent of respondents viewed U.S. leadership as "undesirable."[4]

The status of the city of Kirkuk in northern Iraq presents a second potentially explosive problem. Kirkuk sits on top one of the world's largest oil deposits. Turkish officials fear that control of Kirkuk and its oil wealth by the Kurdistan Regional Government (KRG) would enable the Iraqi Kurds to finance an independent Kurdish state. If the Iraqi Kurds attempt to make Kirkuk the capital of their autonomous region, Turkey could be provoked to launch a major ground invasion, which could exacerbate instability in Iraq and the region as a whole.

New Regional Activism.

Turkey's greater activism in the Middle East has also been reflected in its effort to strengthen ties to its regional neighbors, particularly Iran and Syria. Turkey's relations with both countries were strained in the 1980s and 1990s, in part because they supported the PKK against Turkey. However, relations with Tehran and Damascus have significantly improved in recent years.

Concerns about the impact of rising Kurdish nationalism have been a major driving force behind Turkey's rapprochement with both countries. Iran and Syria have Kurdish minorities on their own territory. They share Turkey's interest in containing Kurdish nationalism and preventing the emergence of an independent Kurdish state on their own borders. This has provided an important incentive for both countries to cooperate more closely with Ankara.

Energy has also been a major driver behind the warming of Turkey's ties to Iran. Iran is the second largest supplier of natural gas to Turkey after Russia. In July 1996 shortly after taking office, Turkish Prime

Minister Necmettin Erbakan concluded a $23 billion natural gas deal with Iran. The deal set the framework for long-term delivery of natural gas for the following 25 years. Since then, energy ties have continued to strengthen.

Relations with Syria have sharply improved in the last decade. Like Turkey, Syria faces an internal problem with its Kurdish minority, which has shown increasing signs of restlessness. The Baathist leadership around President Bashar Assad has been concerned that the emergence of an economically robust Kurdish government in northern Iraq could stimulate pressures for economic and political improvements among Syria's Kurdish population and pose a challenge to the regime's stability. These concerns have been a prime driver behind the growing cooperation between Ankara and Damascus.

Ankara's diplomatic engagement in the Lebanon crisis in the summer and fall of 2006 provides another example of Turkey's new activism in the Middle East. The Erdogan government's decision to send 1,000 troops to participate in the United Nations (UN) peace-keeping force in Lebanon represented an important departure from Turkey's traditional policy of avoiding deep involvement in Middle Eastern affairs and provoked a heated internal debate in Turkey. Such an action would have been unthinkable a few years ago, thus underscoring Turkey's readiness to play a much more active role in the Middle East lately.

The Israeli Connection.

Turkey's policy toward Israel has also undergone an important shift. The Erdogan government has pursued a much more active benign Palestinian policy than its predecessors. Erdogan has been openly critical of Israeli actions in the West Bank and Gaza, calling them acts of "state terror."[5] These remarks caused irritation in Jerusalem and contributed to strains in Turkey's bilateral ties with Israel.

At the same time, Turkey has sought to establish closer ties to the Palestinian leadership. A few weeks after the elections in the Palestinian territories, Turkey hosted a high-ranking Hamas delegation led by Khaled Mashaal in Ankara. The visit was arranged without consultation with the United States or Israel, provoking strong anger in Washington and Jerusalem because it directly undercut U.S. and Israeli efforts to isolate Hamas until it met a series of specific conditions, including acknowledgment of Israel's right to exist.

Turkey's approach to the crisis in Lebanon provides another example where Turkey has adopted an independent position at odds with Israeli policy. Erdogan sharply condemned the Israeli attacks, declaring that they in no way could be considered legitimate.[6] The attacks prompted large-scale protests and the burning of the Israeli flag in several major Turkish cities. A number of nongovernmental organizations also issued statements condemning Israeli policies in Lebanon and the Palestinian territories.

Implications for U.S. Policy.

U.S. policymakers will need to get used to dealing with a more independent-minded and assertive Turkey, one increasingly inclined to pursue its own interests. This will particularly affect the ability of the United States to use Turkish military facilities for operations in the Middle East. Turkey is likely to be extremely wary of allowing the United States to use its military facilities for operations in the Middle East and Gulf except in cases where these operations clearly serve NATO or Turkish national interests.

Relations with Iran and Syria represent another area where adjustments are needed. Turkey has a strong and enduring interest in maintaining good relations with both countries. Pressuring Turkey to curtail these ties or isolate either country will not work and will only exacerbate strains in relations with Ankara. Rather than seeing Turkey's ties to Tehran and Damascus as a problem, Washington should view them as an asset. As a close neighbor with historical ties to the region, Turkey can act as a useful interlocutor at a time when U.S. ties to Iran and Syria are strained.

Finally—and most important—Washington needs to address Turkish concerns about PKK terrorism more resolutely. Washington should press the Kurdish Regional Government in Northern Iraq to crack down on PKK activities and close the PKK training camps on its soil. Second, it should insist that the Kurdish government in Northern Iraq arrest and turn over to the Turkish government key PKK leaders, many of whom continue to roam freely in northern Iraq and even appear on Kurdish television stations supported by the Kurdish autonomous government. Such a move would have a dramatic psychological impact in Turkey and do much to reduce the growing anti-Americanism among the Turkish population.

ENDNOTES - CHAPTER 6

1. Suat Kiniklioglu, "Let Turkey be Turkey," *Today's Zaman*, February 14, 2007.

2. According to Turkish estimates, Turkey's support in enforcing sanctions against Iraq cost Turkey $6 billion and the cost of deploying 100,000 troops another $300 million.

3. Ian Lesser, "Turkey, the United States, and the Geo-Politics of Delusion," *Survival,* Vol. 48, No. 3, Fall 2006, p. 2.

4. See *Transatlantic Trends: Key Findings 2006,* Washington, DC: German Marshall Fund of the United States, 2006, p. 19.

5. "Israeli Operation Draws Ire in Turkey," *The Probe,* May 23, 2004; "Turkey Irked by Gaza Offensive But Not Prompted to Reverse Ties to Israel," *The Probe,* May 30, 2004.

6. "Erdogan: Unfair War in Lebanon Will Have No Winner," *Turkish Daily News,* August 4, 2006.

CHAPTER 7

THE NEW MIDDLE EAST, TURKEY, AND THE SEARCH FOR REGIONAL STABILITY

Gökhan Çetinsaya

A new Middle East is emerging since the U.S. invasion of Iraq in March 2003. The developments in Iraq will have far-reaching consequences for the region's future. Iraq is like a miniature of the Middle East with its population structure, social characteristics, religious mixture, problems, and challenges. A process of reciprocal influence is to be expected between Iraq and its neighbors. Each domestic actor in Iraq has relations with ethnic and religious groups in the neighboring countries. The Kurds in northern Iraq have links with the Kurds in Syria, Turkey, and Iran; the Shiite Arabs have relations with Arab and non-Arab Shiites in Iran, Kuwait, Bahrain, and Saudi Arabia; the Sunni Arabs have relations with the Sunni Arabs in Syria and Jordan, and with Islamic movements in the Arab world; and the Turcomans have relations with Turkey. All the neighboring and regional countries also have interest in and relations with these groups and actors in Iraq. Therefore, the developments in Iraq will affect neighboring countries, while policies pursued by its neighbors will inevitably have an impact on Iraq.

The New Middle East.

The new Middle East seems to take its shape in the light of the following interrelated trends:
- There is a rise of nonstate actors in the Middle East. They appear (as witnessed in Iraq, Lebanon,

and Palestine) to play crucial roles in the region. They have their own armed militias; they fight with the national armies; and they challenge the states.

- There are at the same time ethnic and sectarian groups. Both at the state and nonstate levels, ethnic and sectarian groups are rising as new influential actors, and ethnic and sectarian discourse and politics will be dominant in the region.
- There are also "Islamist" groups. "Islamism" or "Political Islam" will be influential as a political power. The "Islamist" trend includes both armed and nonarmed groups, as well as both Shiite and Sunni groups.
- A new strategic balance of power in the Middle East is emerging. The results of the loss of Iraq's strong army and its "Arab identity" in the region will be enormous. Iraq, as a powerful Arab country, has withdrawn from the regional equation, and Iran, Israel, and Turkey will aim to fill the strategic vacuum. The new Iraq, as a militarily weak and politically unstable country, changes the balance of power in the region especially at the expense of the Arab world.
- In this new strategic environment, there has been much discussion on the emergence of a "Shiite crescent" in the region. In fact, there appears to be emerging not one but three crescents in the new Middle East:

1. **The Shiite crescent.** The new Iraq turns out to be a country in which the Shiite Arabs may dominate both the central government and foreign policy in the federal and democra-

tic processes as prescribed by the constitution. It is inevitable that in such a situation Iran will gain an enormous advantage. The economic, social, cultural, and religious interactions between the two countries that had been stymied by the Ba'ath regime will definitely increase in this new era. These interactions will cause anxiety for other regional actors, who think that a "Shiite crescent" is being created in the region stretching from Pakistan to Lebanon. Shiites comprise 60 percent of the population in Bahrain, 40 percent in Kuwait, 14 percent in Saudi Arabia, and 35 percent in Lebanon. In some analyses, the Zaydis who comprise 73 percent of the population in Yemen and the Nusayris in Syria, who remain outside the Twelver Shiite Islam, are also added to the crescent. This political-religious crescent is at the same time an "oil crescent" under Shiite control, stretching across Iran, Bahrain, the eastern province of Saudi Arabia, and southern Iraq. In addition to the aforementioned geopolitical-economic-religious factors, one should also expect the effects of social and cultural changes from the process of globalization in the Shiite world.

2. **The Muslim Brotherhood crescent.** The new Middle East has witnessed the rise of the Muslim Brotherhood parties in different parts of the region. The parties which adopted the political, social, and religious philosophy of the Muslim Brotherhood movement are gaining strength in Sunni Arab politics day by day. In countries like Palestine, where democratic elections were allowed, these

parties won the elections. In other countries like Egypt and Jordan, where democratic elections were not allowed, they became main opposition parties.

3. **The Kurdish crescent.** The developments in northern Iraq will inevitably have political, social, economic, and cultural impacts on the Kurds living in Turkey, Iran, and Syria, all neighboring countries. Both in the short and the long run, these countries will feel the impact of the "Kurdish Federal Region," which was established in northern Iraq. The rise of the idea of independence and a pan-Kurdish movement should be expected to gather momentum, especially among the post-1991 generations in northern Iraq. In addition to mutual political effects, we should also expect social, cultural, and economic interplay due to strong tribal and religious relations across the borders. Cultural interaction will have wider dimensions given the opportunities of globalization, i.e., news media, universities, newspapers, magazines, other literary products, and internet facilities. A significant economic interaction should also be expected in this crescent, especially between Turkey and northern Iraq.

Turkey and the New Middle East.

In this new Middle East, Turkey faces several challenges, risks, and opportunities. Turkey is extremely anxious over the regional ferment discussed above, and tries to pursue a careful and comprehensive diplomacy in the region in order to forestall consequent adverse developments. Turkish political and military elites believe that the disintegration of Iraq and/or new destabilizations in the Middle East could be disastrous for the region as well as Turkey.

What is Turkey's current policy toward the Middle East? Turkey's position can be understood only in the context of the general foreign policy and strategic vision of the new Turkish foreign policy decisionmakers or the Justice and Development Party (JDP) elites. In their vision, Turkey has become a pivotal country and a regional power in Eurasia and the Middle East since the end of the Cold War, with great potential for playing a constructive role and also even the potential to become a global actor. This vision, which denies a mere "bridge" role for Turkey, sets forth four main principles of Turkish foreign policy. The first principle is to establish a link between freedom and security. After September 11, 2001 (9/11), the world led by the United States became urgently preoccupied with security, largely at the expense of freedom. The only exception in this context has been Turkey: Only Turkey after 9/11 achieved freedom and democratization at the same time; only Turkey adopted a further democratization program without risking its security, both in internal and external politics.

The second principle might be called "zero-problems with the neighbors." According to this injunction, rather than viewing neighboring countries as enemies or potential enemies, or adopting a defensive attitude towards neighbors, Turkey should aim to establish good relations with all of its neighbors. By implementing this principle, Turkey will gain extraordinary room for maneuver in the region. Such an orientation is also the first prerequisite for Turkey to become a pivotal state or a key player in the Middle East.

The third principle is to establish a multidimensional and multitrack foreign policy, which also entails

Turkey's assumption of a new pivotal role in the Greater Middle East region. In today's international and regional dynamics, Turkey cannot maintain a static or one-dimensional foreign policy, but instead should pursue multiple tracks. Accordingly, for example, it is not a contradiction to create joint ventures with both Russia and the United States, or both the United States and the European Union (EU). It is not a contradiction to establish close relations with its neighbors and maintain strategic relations with the United States. Turkey can discuss the problems and create solutions in the East, without denying its western identity. At the same time, Turkey can adopt western values and principles and can discuss the future of Europe from a European perspective, without denying its Eastern identity. In this way, Turkey can also contribute to the EU's bid to become a global power, instead of a continental power. This vision sees all these joint or multidimensional relations as different parts of a unified Big Picture, much like viewing the global system as a giant jigsaw puzzle in which Turkey seeks its proper position vis-à-vis the positions of its neighbors, friends, and allies.

The final principle is to pursue a proactive and visionary foreign policy, instead of a passive, reactive, or defensive foreign policy. Turkey, as a regional power and a pivotal country, should formulate and pursue a proactive, constructive, and comprehensive foreign policy that does not shrink from taking prudent initiatives. In the new international and regional environment, Turkey should not become a source of problems, but a problem-solving country, and should take initiatives to solve the problems of its region.

Turkish-American Interests in the Middle East.

The "Shared Vision and Structured Dialogue to Advance the Turkish-American Strategic Partnership" document, dated July 5, 2006, posits that Turkey and the United States "share the same set of values and ideals in our regional and global objectives: the promotion of peace, democracy, freedom, and prosperity." Turkey and the United States pledge themselves to work together on all issues of common concern, including,

- promoting peace and stability in the broader Middle East through democracy;
- supporting international efforts towards a permanent settlement of the Arab-Israeli conflict, including international efforts to resolve the Israeli-Palestinian conflict on the basis of a two-state solution;
- fostering stability, democracy, and prosperity in a unified Iraq;
- supporting diplomatic efforts regarding Iran's nuclear program, including the recent P5+1 initiative;
- contributing to stability, democracy, and prosperity in the Black Sea region, the Caucasus, Central Asia, and Afghanistan;
- supporting the achievement of a just, lasting, comprehensive, and mutually acceptable settlement of the Cyprus question under the auspices of the UN, and in this context ending the isolation of the Turkish Cypriots;
- enhancing energy security through diversification of routes and sources, including from the Caspian basin;

- strengthening transatlantic relations and the transformation of the North Atlantic Treaty Organization (NATO);
- countering terrorism, including the fight against the Partiya Karkeren Kurdistan (Kurdish Workers Party or PKK) and its affiliates;
- preventing proliferation of weapons of mass destruction (WMD);
- combating illegal trafficking of persons, drugs, and weapons;
- increasing understanding, respect, and tolerance between and among religions and cultures; and
- promoting effective multilateral action to find solutions to international challenges and crises of common concern.

Looking at this lengthy list, we perceive that the majority of U.S. and Turkish interests seem to be converging. But there are differences in perspectives concerning the realization of these interests. In other words, the aims are identical, but the means are conflicting.

The case of the Broader Middle East and North Africa Initiative (BMEI) is illuminating. In principle, the ruling JDP elites support the U.S. BMEI project as an essential initiative for the future good of the Middle East. This vision accepts globalization as a natural stage of world history, and it is not surprising to see the effects of globalization in the Middle East already occurring. Globalization will thus manifest itself fully in the Middle East sooner or later, regardless of the U.S. initiative. The transformation towards democratization in the Middle East is less secure. It should have begun 10 years ago at the end of the Cold War, as in Eastern European countries. It did not happen then for several reasons, but it should certainly start now. The Middle East cannot survive for very long with its present political systems, and should therefore adopt democratic values and structures, and integrate itself into the global system. But the JDP elites find reason to criticize the method or style of implementation of the initiative by the Bush administration.

For Turkish elites, there are two main stipulations with regard to implementation of the American initiative. First, the initiative should not change the political landscape of the Middle East. It should not fragment or dissolve existing nation-states or alter their current borders. This would lead to chaos in the region. Second, the implementation should emerge from within the existing framework of each national system and people, and should take social, cultural, and economic parameters of each regional member into account. This new Turkish foreign policy vision argues that a self-confident Turkey should formulate and develop its own project in terms of the BMEI, and implement it within its own parameters. Then, according to this vision, Turkey could manage great transformations in the region without foreign intervention. In this regard, Turkey should have an active policy for the future of the region, prepare the conceptual framework for this initiative, share it with the people of the region, and transform the region even as it maintains peace and stability.

The Turkish elites also have reservations with respect to U.S. intentions vis-à-vis Iran. Like the United States, Turkey is against the nuclearization of Iran. A nuclear Iran would change the strategic balance between the two countries and in the region at the expense of Turkey's national security interests. But Turkish political and military elites are also against

U.S. military intervention in Iran. First, Turkey does not want another war and another round of destabilization along its borders in the mold of developments in Iraq since 2003. Second, such intervention could entail great economic costs for Turkey, as well as direct military threats to its security. Turkish elites argue that a foreign military intervention in Iran would lead to destabilization and disintegration of Iran, and that this would strengthen Kurdish nationalism or facilitate the establishment of an independent Kurdish state. Ankara and Tehran collaborated on the Kurdish issue from the 1930s until the mid-1960s, and now they are in full collaboration on the issue of PKK terrorism. In other words, Turkey sees the possibility of a nuclear Iran as a long-term threat; however, the most salient short-term threat in the eyes of Turkish political and military elites is PKK terrorism, along with the possibility of a Kurdish state in northern Iraq. On all these shorter-term issues, Turkey needs the help or support of Iran.

As if all the foregoing Turkish concerns were not enough, it appears that in recent months a new division has emerged in the Middle East between the so-called radicals (the anti-American actors Iran, Syria, Hamas, Hezbollah) and the so-called moderates (pro-American Saudi Arabia, Egypt, Jordan, Kuwait). The two sides struggle for power over Iraq, Lebanon, and Palestine, and both sides fight proxy wars. In this new picture, all groups look to Turkey, and all groups want Turkey in their camp. But Turkey is extremely anxious over these developments in the region. What does Turkey want? Turkey does not want confrontation or a new cold war in the Middle East between the Shiites and Sunnis, or pro-Americans and anti-Americans. Turkey wants an engaging dialogue, security-building measures, peace, stability, cooperation, and integration. Turkey wants to play a constructive, facilitating, and balancing role in the new Middle East. Turkey wants to establish balanced and equal relations with all actors on all levels. Turkey argues that relations based on confrontation should be abandoned. Instead, an active, constructive, and multidimensional policy which emphasizes peace, security, democracy, and stability should be developed. To this effect, Turkey is ready to pursue a comprehensive public policy towards the people and actors of the region and international actors. Among Turkey's expectations are participatory democracy based on territorial integrity; effective use and fair sharing of resources; ethnic-sectarian integration; pluralism; security for all; constitutions that guarantee basic rights and freedoms; political consensus; and stability. From Turkey's point of view, the new Middle East needs four fundamental features for peace and stability: (1) a regional security system for all; (2) mutual political dialogue; (3) economic integration and interdependence; and (4) cultural pluralism.

A Proposal for Regional Peace and Stability.

The problems in the Middle East are highly complex, interrelated, and intertwined. Negotiation or dialogue between two actors cannot solve regional problems. Therefore, a comprehensive and all-inclusive mechanism is needed to enhance prospects for peace and stability in the Middle East. All regional and global actors (all regional countries plus the UN, UN Security Council, G-8 countries, Organization of Islamic Countries, Gulf Cooperation Council, and the Arab League) should be involved; and all regional problems should be dealt with on the same table at the same time. For this purpose, a new "Helsinki Process" for the Middle East, adapted according to the realities and nature of the region, should be established. Through this mechanism, a process of confidence-building measures, encouragement of political dialogue, economic integration and interdependence, and cultural pluralism in the region might well be achieved.

CHAPTER 8

THE EVOLVING EU, NATO, AND TURKEY RELATIONSHIP

Sinan Ülgen

Turkey's quest to take part fully in transatlantic as well as European security structures remains unresolved due to Cyprus, a problem that undermines the North Atlantic Treaty Organization (NATO)-European Union (EU) relationship with serious ramifications for transatlantic dialogue on strategic security. The Cyprus matter also precludes Turkey's further convergence with the European Security and Defense Policy (ESDP) and creates a genuine dilemma for Turkish policymakers. While NATO remains a fundamental foreign policy pillar for Turkey—and Turkish and U.S. positions on the future of NATO converge—the Alliance remains handicapped by political difficulties that could be partially overcome if Cyprus is resolved. But incentives are lacking for a long-term settlement, a situation that highlights the need for an improvement in the Turkey-U.S. relationship.

Turkey's EU membership process has affected Turkish foreign and security policy, its perception of NATO, and its relationship with the United States in many different ways. The starting point for Turkey can be characterized as the quest to maintain NATO's role as the primary institution for security and defense in Europe and as the main forum for transatlantic cooperation, while carving out a role for itself within the burgeoning sphere of European security and defense. Turkey achieved a considerable degree of success a decade ago by obtaining virtual member status within the Western European Union (WEU). This achievement proved, however, to be of a temporary nature. The St. Malo agreement of 1998 between the United Kingdom (UK) and France, which paved the way for the development of a ESDP within the EU structures, meant the dissolution of the WEU as the security arm of the EU. It also meant the sudden disappearance of all the hard-fought *acquis* (attainments) that provided the foundation of the security relationship between Turkey and the EU.

Since then, the security relationship between Turkey and the EU has had to be redefined. This exercise proved to be a difficult and strenuous one, and the process has been significantly influenced by the internal political dynamics within an EU intent on determining the limits of the *communautairization* ("communitization") of defense and security policy. The concomitant process of enlargement, and the constitutional debacle which ushered in a new period of reflection on the future of Europe, further muddled the picture. Finally, the lingering uncertainty about Turkish accession provided another layer of volatility. Indeed, policymakers have had to negotiate the current institutional arrangements between Turkey and the EU member states in the field of security and defense cooperation without knowing whether they were temporary or permanent. Had there been a clear political will on the EU side for supporting Turkey's full membership objective, Turkish policymakers may have been more flexible with regard to their demands, knowing that these arrangements would necessarily be upgraded once Turkey became a full member.

As things stand, the Turkey-EU relationship in the security domain is still fraught with difficulty.

Turkey's aspirations to become a full-fledged contributor to Europe's security, with rights nearly equal
to those of EU full members, remain unfulfilled. In
particular, Turkey wants to be fully associated with
the planning and implementation of EU-led missions,
as opposed to being asked for its contribution if and
when needed and after the political and technical
planning phase is completed. Such full association is
how Turkish policymakers define the characteristics of
a genuine partnership in this sphere. They also believe
that if these conditions were to hold, Turkey could
substantially reinforce the EU's military and civilian
crisis management capacities. Furthermore, the last
EU enlargement, which brought in the Republic of
Cyprus, creates a new set of problems, not only for the
Turkey-EU relationship, but also for the EU-NATO
relationship.

The central problem for the EU-NATO relationship
can be traced back to the interpretation of the agreement
between NATO and the EU, reached at the end of 2002.
It basically sealed the decision made by NATO at the
Washington Summit to provide support to the EU
under "Berlin Plus" in exchange for certain rights within
the ESDP for non-EU European allies, as stipulated in
the Nice implementation document. Non-Partnership
for Peace (PfP) countries and those lacking a security
agreement are excluded by the NATO decision from
activities, including discussions, related to **both** Berlin
Plus and strategic partnership. The EU decision,
however, limits the exclusion **only** to Berlin Plus and
does not refer to strategic cooperation. Therefore, under
the NATO decision, Cyprus is excluded (along with
Malta) from participating in any activity falling under
"strategic cooperation." This is not the case, however,
according to the EU decision. Today, the EU seeks to

overcome the problems posed by this wording. On the basis of the EU solidarity principle, the EU claims that Cyprus can no longer be left outside the scope of this arrangement and refuses to engage in dialogue with NATO without all EU members sitting around the table.

As a result, while there is an agreed mechanism to do so, there is practically no meaningful dialogue between NATO and the EU on emerging threats. EU-NATO strategic cooperation remains blocked. The agenda of the regularly scheduled joint meetings of the North Atlantic Council (NAC) and the EU Political and Security Committee (PSC) are generally void of any new items and can legitimately discuss only the Berlin Plus operation in Bosnia. Questions of imminent concern, such as the fight against terrorism and energy security, cannot be tackled.

This state of affairs can also negatively impact performance in the theater of operations. The need for strategic cooperation will become more pressing as the EU prepares to replace the UN in Kosovo and undertakes a rule of law mission in Afghanistan. In both of these areas, NATO's military presence will coexist with EU civilian missions. The existing collaboration in the field between the two institutions cannot remedy the lack of cooperative interaction at the policy level in the headquarters. This predicament will be increasingly visible if and when the situation on the ground, especially in Afghanistan or Kosovo, becomes crisis prone. In short, the uncertainties linked to Turkey's EU accession and the intractable problem of Cyprus have created serious detriments to a genuine and substantive NATO-EU partnership.

The inability or unwillingness of some EU member states to think constructively about the institutional arrangements linking Turkey to the ESDP creates a dilemma for Turkish policymakers. On the one hand, on almost all issues related to regional security (with the notable exception of the Cyprus problem), Turkish policy is actually quite closely aligned with European foreign policy. It is perhaps worth recalling that Turkey's alignment with Common Foreign and Security Policy (CFSP) statements and common positions stands at 92 percent.

Turkey has participated in a number of military and civilian ESDP missions including those in Macedonia (two) and the Congo. It is currently participating in missions in Bosnia (two) and Kinshasa. Turkey is also slated to participate in the EU-led Kosovo police mission as well. Indeed, it is the most active participant in ESDP missions among all third countries and outperforms many EU member states as well. It is the sixth largest contributor to the Althea mission in Bosnia, for instance. In addition, Turkey makes regular commitments to the EU's headline goals by specifying the different military assets to be incorporated in the catalogue of EU forces. Turkey is also set to become a contributor to the Italian-led EU battlegroup to be established in the second half of 2010.

Furthermore, Turkish security doctrine is more at ease with the approach outlined in the EU security strategy than with U.S. security strategy. References to effective multilateralism, soft power, and critical dialogue contrast with the more robust and direct approach of the United States to regional security, as illustrated particularly in Iraq and as feared in some quarters in relation to Iran. With its growing political and economic influence and self-confidence, Turkey has become more active in regional politics. Its relationship with the countries of the Middle East has improved considerably. Trade and investment flows between Turkey and the region are at an all-time high. Therefore, there would be significant opportunity costs for Turkey of a radical change in the *status quo* in the region. In that sense, Turkey is a regional status quo power. Whereas the EU is perceived as a more conservative foreign policy actor, the United States is seen as an impatiently proactive power that sometimes acts without giving measured consideration to where all the chips may fall. It may be useful to recall that one of the main stumbling blocks during the Turkey-U.S. negotiations in February 2003 before the ill-fated vote of the Turkish parliament on the opening of a new northern front in Iraq, was the inability of the U.S. administration to spell out convincingly to Turkish authorities what the U.S. exit strategy for Iraq was. The dilemma for Turkish authorities is therefore a very fundamental one. From a policy perspective, the natural ally seems increasingly to be the EU. But institutional and political realities preclude the elaboration of a mutually satisfactory framework for the deepening of the Turkey-EU security cooperation.

On the foreign policy front, the Turkey-EU relationship has not progressed as one would have hoped. The reason is the difficulties brought about by the start of the accession negotiations. Whereas the initiation of negotiations had been expected to usher in a period of increased mutual trust, confidence, and therefore collaboration, the real as well as imaginary barriers erected in Europe against Turkey's full membership have prevented such an outcome. As a result, foreign policy cooperation and dialogue between Turkey and the EU remains below its potential. The frequency, scope, and format of the currently existing framework for the exchange of views on regional issues such as Iran, Iraq, and the Caucasus, and even in the area of energy security, are clearly insufficient for a genuine policy dialogue and partnership to emerge between Turkey and the EU.

Given this state of affairs, Turkey's outlook on NATO and on evolving U.S.-Turkey relations acquires more importance. As regards NATO, Turkey has traditionally been a very Atlanticist nation. The sharing of a long border with the former enemy was surely a factor in this regard. Now that the Cold War is over, NATO's importance for Turkey remains undiminished: NATO is the essential security organization for Turkey. Furthermore Turkey's absence from the EU's security structures serves to underscore NATO's uniqueness.

Moreover, NATO's agenda is pretty much aligned with the priorities of Turkish foreign policy. Almost all issues taken up by the North Atlantic Council relate to areas of direct concern to Turkey. In other words, there is a definite convergence between NATO's policies and Turkish foreign policy. Given that the NATO map of threat assessments focuses on regions in Turkey's neighborhood, this symmetry is likely to be sustained in the longer term as well. One might therefore claim that Turkey finds NATO working on its top "hard security" priorities whereas the EU appears to focus on a more comprehensive agenda involving "soft security."

Turkey formulates its policy regarding the future of NATO against this backdrop. The Turkish position is very similar to the U.S. position as regards the future of the Alliance. Turkey believes that NATO is essentially a political and military organization and that, as such, its role is not limited to purely military matters. In other words, NATO should be a platform for Alliance members to discuss global and regional political developments that have a bearing on the security of NATO members. Turkey also believes that in addition to hard security, NATO could potentially play a role in providing soft security in crisis areas by enhancing its civilian crisis management capabilities. This is, however, a contentious issue between the United States and some European members of the Alliance, who are resisting all efforts to steer the Alliance towards these objectives. For those countries, NATO is a purely military organization with no role to play in furthering political dialogue on regional issues. By the same token, civilian crisis management falls under the responsibility of the EU. Hence a clear division of tasks between the EU and NATO is to be followed, in which the EU should be the primary organization for civilian crisis management.

Ironically, even though Turkey shares the U.S. view on the future of NATO, the obstruction of NATO-EU strategic cooperation due to the Cyprus problem plays in favor of those countries that have a less ambitious vision for the future of the Alliance and a preference for the EU to build up its own civilian crisis management capabilities. In other words, because the two institutions cannot officially discuss the strategy for new ventures, NATO remains stuck in its present ambit. The institutional bottleneck caused by the question of Cyprus also serves to conceal the deep rift between the United States and some of the European members of NATO on NATO's role and future. As a consequence, if these divisions are not remedied, the fear is that the United States will cease to view NATO as a useful organization. The outcome would then be the weakening of the transatlantic link in the security domain and a more definite shift of U.S. policy towards unilateralism or at best bilateralism.

Turkey is therefore under increased pressure from its European allies to accept the new state of affairs and lift its veto on Cyprus. So far, Turkey has conditionally decided to lift its objection to the NATO-EU strategic dialogue with the EU-27, i.e., including Cyprus. The conditions require that the meetings be held nonofficially (i.e., "informal" dialogues) and only in relation to urgent matters involving humanitarian concerns. As a result of this relaxation of attitude, informal NAC-PSC meetings were held on Darfur and on Kosovo.

Turkish officials are undoubtedly aware of the detrimental consequences for the Alliance as a whole of their blocking the conclusion of Cyprus' security agreement with NATO. Technically, it is the absence of such an agreement which prevents Cyprus from taking part in the EU-NATO strategic dialogue. The other condition is Cyprus' participation in PfP. However, this is a strategically and politically sensitive decision for Turkey. It is seen as the sole real leverage that Turkey has on the Papadopoulos regime in Greece. It must be recalled that Cyprus (and Greece) are blocking Turkey's security agreement and its participation in the European Defense Agency (EDA), even though Norway, another non-EU NATO member, is allowed to participate fully in EDA. The Cypriot government is intent on using Turkey's negotiations process to steal concessions from Turkey regarding a political settlement on the island. For Turkish policymakers, the NATO card remains an indispensable element in their efforts to redress this asymmetric relationship.

The international community has so far been unable to induce the Papadopoulos government to continue the UN-sponsored negotiations on Cyprus in good faith. The incentives for the Greek Cypriots to adopt a conciliatory stance are lacking. They are comforted by their internationally recognized status, and their EU membership gives them additional confidence. So unless a serious commitment is made by the international community to support the UN process and create the right incentives for the Greek Cypriots to reach a mutually satisfactory agreement with the Turkish Cypriots, Turkey will most likely continue to block any initiative for Cyprus to conclude a security agreement with NATO. As a matter of fact, this is perhaps not more than an annoyance for the Greek Cypriots. The Greek Cypriot government may eventually be unwilling or find it politically impossible to apply for NATO partnership. But, at the least, the present state of affairs serves to underscore the existence of an international problem and raises the specter of possible contagion in other areas. Therefore, it may induce the transatlantic community to become more actively involved in the resolution of this specific conflict.

The United States will be a key player in this effort. Yet, U.S. policy on Cyprus will greatly depend on the evolution of Turkey-U.S. relations, which nowadays are dominated by the quagmire that Iraq has become. Should the Iraqi question as well as the PKK issue start to shed their dominant influence on the bilateral relationship, new areas of cooperation between the United States and Turkey in the global and regional security field can be explored with a renewed spirit of cooperation. Turkish policy could then be more attuned to the needs of the transatlantic community. It should be recalled that whenever Turkish forces are to be sent abroad to participate in a UN- or NATO-led peacekeeping or peace enforcement mission, the main criticism heard from the body politic is, How can

Turkey spare these forces while it is waging a fight against armed terrorists on its home turf? In that sense, Turkey is indeed in a unique position among Alliance members as a country faced with terrorism in the form of guerrilla warfare. That is why Turkey's military contributions to recent peacekeeping operations have not been commensurate with its actual capabilities.

Turkey's contributions to peacekeeping and peace enforcement operations, be they under the UN or NATO umbrella or as part of a "coalition of the willing," will also be affected by the political climate between Turkey and the United States. If that climate is poor, we can expect Turkey to be less forthcoming to the extent that these missions are led by the United States or are identified as fulfilling a U.S. foreign policy objective.

To conclude, what specific measures should be taken to overcome the problems highlighted in this analysis?

- **The Cyprus issue must be addressed.** The negative impact of the ongoing dispute in Cyprus cannot be overemphasized. Since Cyprus joined the EU, the contagion potential of this regional dispute in the political and security field has been very clear. The NATO-EU relationship was effectively hindered. More active involvement of the United States will be critical in the search for a lasting settlement. Indeed, with Cyprus having gained EU membership, the United States, as a non-EU member of the P-5 of the UN Security Council, can be instrumental in creating the proper incentives to budge the Papadopoulos government. For what it is worth, we should note that the new president of Cyprus, Demetris Christofias, has issued a public pledge "to restart moribund talks to reunify the island and [has] agreed to meet the leader of the breakaway Turkish Cypriots."[1]

- **Turkey and the EU must engage in a program of confidence building.** The normalization of the NATO-EU relationship will depend to a great extent on the normalization of the Turkey-EU relationship, which in turn depends on two factors. The first one is Cyprus. As long as the dispute remains unresolved, Turkey's EU aspirations will remain on hold. The second factor is the EU's approach to Turkey. Notwithstanding the question of Cyprus, the EU has been unable to send the right messages to its putative future member and negotiating partner. For instance, the "privileged partner" rhetoric (i.e., in lieu of membership) refuses to abate. The possibility of national referenda in some member states on Turkish accession is a further difficulty clouding the road to full membership. Under these conditions, Turkish policymakers and Turkish public opinion continue to nurture doubts about the country's ability ever to fulfill the conditions for full membership. EU member states must now simply allow Turkey to proceed with the negotiations on the same basis as past candidates. In addition, European institutions as well as national governments should take more responsibility in communicating with their publics about enlargement, with a view to building a more solid foundation for eventual accession.

- **Finally, even if the Cyprus obstacle is lifted, the NATO-EU relationship may still stumble as a result of the deep divisions regarding** the future of NATO between the Atlanticist members of the Alliance and the others. Therefore, the rejuvenation of the transatlantic dialogue, which seems to have started after the French presidential elections, will hopefully result in a more constructive debate about the division of tasks between NATO and the EU.

ENDNOTES - CHAPTER 8

1. "Cyprus Elects Communist President," *Washington Post,* February 25, 2008, p. A9.

ABOUT THE CONTRIBUTORS

FRANCES G. BURWELL is Vice President, Director of Transatlantic Relations and Studies at the Atlantic Council of the United States. Her areas of expertise include U.S.-EU relations and the development of the European Union's foreign and defense policies, as well as NATO and a range of transatlantic economic and political issues. She is the author of *The Indispensable Partnership: Launching a New NATO-EU Relationship in Riga* and the co-author of *Law and the Lone Superpower: Rebuilding a Transatlantic Consensus on International Law,* and *Transatlantic Transformation: Building a New NATO-EU Security Architecture.* She has also served as rapporteur for several Atlantic Council policy papers, including *Transatlantic Leadership for a New Global Economy, Changing Terms of Trade: Managing the Transatlantic Economy, The Post-9/11 Partnership: Transatlantic Cooperation against Terrorism,* and *The New Partnership: Building Russia-West Cooperation on Strategic Challenges.* Her articles have also appeared in such publications as *Eurofuture* and the *Wall Street Journal (Europe),* and she has appeared on CNN International and al-Jazeera. She is the co-editor of *The United States and Europe in the Global Arena.* Prior to joining the Council, Dr. Burwell was executive director of the Center for International and Security Studies at the University of Maryland, and also served as founding executive director of Women In International Security. She holds a Ph.D. in Government and Politics from the University of Maryland, an M.Phil. from Oxford University, and a B.A. from Mount Holyoke College.

GÖKHAN ÇETINSAYA is a Professor of History and International Relations at Istanbul Technical University, Department of Humanities and Social Sciences. He is currently a Fellow at the Woodrow Wilson International Center for Scholars (September 2007-May 2008). He works on Turkish political history, Turkish foreign policy, and the Middle East. Dr. Çetinsaya's publications include "A Tale of Two Centuries: Continuities in Turkish Foreign and Security Policy," Nursin Atesoglu-Guney, ed., *Contentious Issues of Security and the Future of Turkey* (London: Ashgate, 2007), pp. 5-18; "The New Iraq, The Middle East and Turkey: A Turkish View" (SETA Report, April 2006, *www.setav.org*); "Turkey's Stature as a Middle Eastern Power," Bruce Maddy-Weitzman and Asher Susser, eds., *Turkish-Israeli Relations in a Trans-Atlantic Context: Wider Europe and the Greater Middle East* (Tel Aviv University, The Moshe Dayan Center for Middle Eastern and African Studies, 2005), pp. 45-50; "The Caliph and Mujtahids: Ottoman Policy towards the Shi'i Community of Iraq in the Late Nineteenth Century," *Middle Eastern Studies*, Vol. 41 (July 2005), pp. 561-574; "Essential Friends and Natural Enemies: The Historical Roots of Turkish-Iranian Relations," *Middle East Review of International Affairs* (September 2003); *Ottoman Administration of Iraq, 1890-1908* (London: Routledge, 2006). Dr. Çetinsaya holds a B.A. and M.A. from the Faculty of Political Sciences at Ankara University and a Ph.D. from the the Department of Middle Eastern Studies at Manchester University.

MICHAEL JAMES LAKE has had two careers; as a journalist and as a European Union diplomat. He was a journalist for national publications for nearly 20 years. As economics correspondent for *The Scotsman*, he covered Britains's first attempt to join the then European Common Market by British Prime Minister Harold Macmillan and chief negotiator Edward Heath, negotiations which were vetoed by President de Gaulle in 1963. He was diplomatic correspondent for the pre-*Murdoch Sun* (London) covering East–West relations, the European Economic Community, and a wide range of international political and economic relations in many countries. In 1970, Ambassador Lake joined *The Guardian* (London), where he became the chief reporter. For 10 years (1963-73) he was a weekly commentator for the BBC World Service on foreign affairs and a regular participant in live panel discussions. When Britain joined the European Community, Ambassador Lake was one of the first 400 British to be recruited to the European Commission under a fast-track system. During postings in London, New York, Brussels, and Tokyo, he lectured in 29 American states and attended six G-7 Summits. In 1991 he was posted to Ankara as European Union (EU) Ambassador, Head of Representation of the European Commission. During his 7-year appointment, Turkey joined the EU customs union, and an Islamic party which had led the government was banned. Its distant successor has since won two general elections, and has carried out deep and EU-driven reforms in its quest for membership in the EU. Ambassador Lake was transferred to Budapest (1998-2001) as EU ambassador responsible for monitoring Hungary's preparations to join the EU, and for multimillion euro financial assistance programs. Hungary joined the EU in 2004. Since his retirement in 2001, Ambassador Lake has been a consultant, writer, and editor. Most notably, he was the editor of *The EU and Turkey: A Glittering Prize or a Millstone?* published by the Federal Trust in 2005. He is also president of the Turkish Area Studies Group in London.

F. STEPHEN LARRABEE is a Senior Staff member at RAND in Washington, DC, and holds the RAND Corporate Chair in European Security. He has taught at Columbia University, Cornell University, New York University, the Paul Nitze School of Advanced International Studies (SAIS), Georgetown University, George Washington University, and the University of Southern California. Before joining RAND, he served as Vice President and Director of Studies of the Institute of East-West Security Studies in New York from 1983-89, and was a distinguished Scholar in Residence at the Institute from 1989-90. From 1978-81, Dr. Larrabee served on the U.S. National Security Council staff in the White House as a specialist on Soviet-East European affairs and East-West political-military relations. He is author of *NATO's Eastern Agenda in a New Strategic Era* (2003), co-author with Ian Lesser of *Turkish Foreign Policy in an Age of Uncertainty* (2003), co-editor with Zalmay Khalilzad and Ian O. Lesser of *The Future of Turkish-Western Relations* (2000), co-editor with David Gompert of *America and Europe: A Partnership for A New Era* (1997), author of *East European Security After the Cold War,* (1994), editor of *The Volatile Powder Keg: Balkan Security After the Cold War* (1994), co-editor with Robert Blackwill of *Conventional Arms Control and East-West Security* (1989), and editor of *The Two German States and European Security* (1989). Dr. Larrabee holds a Ph.D. in Political Science from Columbia University.

IAN O. LESSER is Senior Transatlantic Fellow in Washington, DC. His expertise includes Transatlantic Relations, NATO, European Union, Turkey, Southern

Europe, North Africa, Mediterranean and Middle Eastern Affairs, North-South Relations, Terrorism, Proliferation, International Security and Geopolitics, and Energy. Dr. Lesser came to GMF in November 2006 from the Woodrow Wilson International Center for Scholars in Washington, DC, where he led a major project on the future of U.S.-Turkish relations. He is also President of Mediterranean Advisors, LLC, and senior advisor to the Luso-American Foundation in Lisbon. Prior to establishing Mediterranean Advisors, Dr. Lesser was Vice President and Director of Studies at the Pacific Council on International Policy in Los Angeles, and spent over a decade at RAND as a senior analyst and research manager specializing in strategic studies and Mediterranean security. From 1994-1995, he was a member of the Secretary's Policy Planning Staff at the US Department of State, where his portfolio included southern Europe, Turkey, and the multilateral track of the Middle East peace process. He is a member of the Council on Foreign Relations, the Atlantic Council of the US, the International Institute for Strategic Studies, the advisory boards of Turkish Policy Quarterly and the International Spectator, and is a former senior fellow of the Onassis foundation. At GMF, Dr. Lesser focuses on Turkey, the US-Turkey-EU triangle, strategies toward North Africa and the Mediterranean, and transatlantic cooperation on new security and public policy challenges. His recent publications include *Iran Policy After the "NIE" – Modest Findings, Revolutionary Effects, Global Trends, Regional Consequences: Wider Strategic Influences on the Black Sea; Beyond Suspicion: Rethinking U.S.-Turkish Relations, From Iran to Israel: American Choices in Iraq; Portugal and the Southern Mediterranean: Transatlantic Interest, and Strategies.* Dr. Lesser was educated at the University of

Pennsylvania, the London School of Economics, and the Fletcher School of Law and Diplomacy, and holds a D.Phil from Oxford University.

O. FARUK LOĞOĞLU is President of the Center for Eurasian Strategic Studies (ASAM), one of the leading think tanks in Turkey, with headquarters in Ankara. In 2006, he retired from public service after 35 years in the Turkish Ministry of Foreign Affairs. Early in his political career, Ambassador Loğoğlu focused on the Middle East and Europe, serving as first secretary on the Turkish Delegation to the European Union (1973-76) and as charge d'affaires in Dhaka, Bangladesh (1976-78). In the 1980s, he focused on bilateral political affairs, in particular Cyprus and Greece, serving as counselor to the permanent representative of Turkey to the United Nations (1980-84) and as consul general in Hamburg, Germany (1986-89). Additionally, he was deputy director general, special advisor to the foreign minister (1989-93) in Ankara, and was appointed Turkey's Ambassador to Copenhagen, Denmark (1993-96) and subsequently transferred to Baku, Azerbaijan (1996-98). Ambassador Loğoğlu was appointed deputy undersecretary for multilateral political affairs in 1998 after his return from Baku. He then served as undersecretary of the foreign ministry from 2000 until his posting as Ambassador of Turkey to the United States in 2001 where he stayed until the end of 2005. He is the author of *İsmet İnönü and the Making of Modern Turkey*, a book about the times and life of the second President of the Turkish Republic. He has published articles on foreign affairs in both Turkish and English languages in different journals. Additionally, he serves as deputy chairman of the Turkish National Commission for UNESCO, as acting president of the Foundation for Local Volunteers for Disaster Relief, and as a member of the board of the Strategic Studies Center of the Turkish Ministry of Foreign Affairs. Ambassador Loğoğlu received a bachelor's degree in political science from Brandeis University and doctorate degree in political science from Princeton University.

W. ROBERT PEARSON heads the International Division of The SPECTRUM Group, a consulting firm in Alexandria, Virginia. He completed a 30-year career in 2006 with the Department of State as Director General of the Foreign Service, responsible for State Department civilian and Foreign Service personnel worldwide. He was U.S. Ambassador to the Republic of Turkey during 2000 to 2003, guiding U.S. relations during a period of economic crisis for Turkey, the war in Afghanistan and the war in Iraq. Prior to that, Ambassador Pearson had assignments as Deputy Chief of Mission at the U.S. Embassy in Paris as well as the U.S. Mission to NATO in Brussels, Executive Secretary of the Department of State, Deputy Executive Secretary of the National Security Council, Deputy Assistant Secretary General of NATO and Chair of NATO's Political Committee, and a Political Officer in China. Before entering the Foreign Service, he served in the Judge Advocate General's Corps in the U.S. Navy. Ambassador Pearson is a graduate of Vanderbilt University and of the University of Virginia School of Law.

SINAN ÜLGEN is chairman of the Turkish think tank, Center for Economics and Foreign Policy Studies. He joined the Turkish Foreign Service in 1990 as a career diplomat and worked for 2 years at the Ministry of

117

Foreign Affairs in Ankara at the United Nations desk. In 1992, he was posted to the Turkish Permanent Delegation to the European Union in Brussels where he took part in the Turkey-EU negotiations on the completion of the customs union. Mr. Ülgen is currently the managing partner of Istanbul Economics, a consultancy focusing on business strategies for EU accession. He is also the author of numerous publications. His research and opinion pieces have been published by the Center for European Policy Studies (CEPS), Center for European Reform (CER), the World Economic Forum, as well as newspapers such as *Le Figaro*, the *Financial Times*, *The Wall Street Journal*, and the *International Herald Tribune*. He is also a foreign affairs columnist for the Turkish daily, *Taraf*. Mr. Ülgen graduated in 1987 from the University of Virginia with a double major in computer sciences and economics and undertook graduate studies at the College of Europe in Brugge, Belgium, where he received a master's degree in European economic integration.